FUN with Oldies
Scott Alan Murphy

THANX

First to my Mom for giving me a Love of Music & Dancing
& letting me follow my dreams wherever they might lead !!!

To fellow DJ Chris Topper for listening to me
go on incessantly about **" Fun with Oldies "**, his moral
support & constructive comments & suggestions, like actually
putting the categories in alphabetical order

& to everyone else I have met in my entire life
(that about covers it !!!)

INTRO

While doing my oldies show "**Scott Alan Murphy's Starlight Ballroom**" on WWZK (Now WILW), Wildwood, New Jersey. I would come up with new & creative ways to put " music sets " together based on a genre like "Teen Idols" or "Girl Groups" or featuring a particular year. Then during "Classic Car Week, Gear Head Ed asked for some CARtoons. CARtoons, I queried ? Yeah, you know, like "Mustang Sally" he answered. So I did a few CAR based songs. Then thanx to Ed on future shows I started doing music sets based on themes & song titles calling it "**Fun with Oldies**" My fans LOVED IT !!!

As time went on, the daily feature took on a life of it's own. I started to get requests for those " themed music sets " from listeners. Certainly a pleasant surprise to me!!! Way C-O-O-L ! I found more & more, what I can only consider as **"Cosmic Connections"** to various selections of the classic oldies & Rock & Roll songs we all knew, sang along to, & loved.

Someone suggested I do a book, so "**Fun with Oldies**" - The Book, was born. I thought I would share this insanity with the radio community & other oldies fanatics who enjoyed my radio show & my having "**Fun with Oldies**"

My other reason for writing this book is totally selfish. I used to carry around these music set ideas on crumpled pieces of paper. Do you know what a crumpled piece of paper looks like after it's washed ?!? Now I've got my book instead! A portable reference & Oldies Book of Lists. Much more durable! & It will be around long after I am gone! Unless, of course, I wash it

The oldies show **Scott Alan Murphy's Starlight Ballroom** concentrated on 50's & 60's Pop & Rock & Roll Oldies, but there are some 70's & 80's, 90's, Blues, & Classic Rock tunes that crept into these listings, as I was writing it, because these classics cuts will definitely be considered oldies by future generations, & somehow seemed appropriate to include,or just because they are personal favorites......like the *Louie Louie Files* or R.E.M.'s - It's the End of the World As We Know It, Jimi Hendrix - All Along the Watchtower or a song by Red Ryder I can definitely relate to called " Lunatic Fringe ".

ENJOY My Book! & Tell Your Friends!
Scott Alan Murphy
.........aka The Veteran Cosmic Rocker
..........aka Murf the Surf

The " Fun with Oldies " Radio Show Format

When I went on vacation a few years ago, my then Program Director, Scott Wahl, asked me to make a playlist of songs they could use to duplicate my show. Since it is an "All Request Show" There is no playlist! ......I pretty much make it up as I go along, based on the requests I get, & play what I think goes together. He insisted!!! I told him. Nobody can do the show exactly like I do, because it's in my head, my zwarped mind. I guess you could say, I pretty much, program the show as I go along. Anything from the Fifties & Sixties!", I said. He insisted even more You know what idiots Program Directors are!?!

OK, OK, This is how it all comes together...If I get a request for Ronettes - " Be My Baby ", I'll follow that up with two more Girl Group Hits,.......The Angels - "My Boyfriend's Back", & the Shangri Las - "Walking in the Sand", for instance,....then "Walking in the Sand" brings to mind The Drifters - "Under The Boardwalk" ....then I might do a double shot with "On Broadway" that ties into the original request, because Phil Spector played the guitar riff in " On Broadway " & also discovered & produced The Ronettes & later married Ronnie Spector. It all ties together in my Free Flow of Consciousness. Elementary, My Dear Watson!!! I could have gone with The Crystals - He's a Rebel & then a Gene Pitney Tune, because he wrote that song. Simple! Cosmic Connections.... my zwarped mind ? It works for me!

The Principal of Three

If you really need guidelines:

When I do dances or parties, I would usually play three slow songs in a row, because it usually takes at least one slow song, for the guys to get up enough nerve to ask the gals to dance & two songs is never enough, ... four just seems like too many.

Three Motown Songs, Three from the "Teen Idols File" or "Girl Groups File" or Three Doo Wop Tunes, or Three songs that take you back to "The Roots of Rock & Roll " or a Three song set from the " Psychedelic Sixties ". It could be something as basic as Three songs from a particular year like 1964.

These music sets are usually inspired by a request, but if I don't get a request I get creative & often go off on a tangent all my own.There is no real formal format, except in my head. Free Flow **Cosmic Connections**.

A Sample **"Fun with Oldies"** music set for **CARtoons** might be

409 - Beach Boys
GTO - Ronnie & Daytonas
Mustang Sally - Wilson Pickett

~ or ~

Beep Beep - Playmates
Pink Cadillac - Aretha Franklin
No Particular Place to Go - Chuck Berry

You Get The Idea!!! A **"Fun with Oldies"** Triple Play !!! It WORKS !!!

The Exception to the Rule

"Fun with Oldies " music sets are usually in triplicate, except in the case of a song from "The Lost Oldies File" which is usually an obscure track, & a one shot deal or a "Double Shot", which is T-W-O. If you are in radio, you should be able to count to three.

Lost Oldies Detective Agency (It's All About The MUSIC)

One of the reasons my show is so popular is my dedication to my listeners. They know I love what I do, & I go to work for them. If I get a request for a song I can't find, I write it down on one of those crumpled pieces of paper I mentioned earlier & put it in my pocket & do everything I can to come up with the song for my next show. So I founded the Lost Oldies Detective Agency.

Sometimes my listeners like to play " Stump the DJ ", so for those really tough requests, I put The " Lost Oldies Detective Agency " on the case. A team of oldies fanatics that congregate on the World Wide Web. (Actually they are locked in my basement, but don't tell anyone)

* Lost Oldies Detective Agency Certified Record Archive Prospectors - You too can join the team & get on my mailing list. Help me find those lost oldies. Send an e-mail to me at this address *funwitholdies@hotmail.com* for info on how to get your Official **L.O.D.A.C.R.A.P.** Certification & Badge. Ok, that's just my zwarped mind once again !!! mindzwarped is a word !!!

Contents

Day
Days of the Week
Dedicated Follower of Fashion
Detectives (See Private Eyes)
Devils (See Angels & Devils)
Dreams & Daydreams
Doctor, Doctor
Dogs (See Pets)
Drugs & Other States of Altered Perception
Eyes Have It
Family Affair
Family Affair - Duos, Brothers, Sisters, Twins
Fire & Smoke
Friends
Food Fight
Fools & Foolish
Garage Rock
Getting Married
Girl Groups
Girl Groups - Motown
Girls
Girl's Names
Girl's Names - Suzie Songs
Girl's Names - Nicknames
Good
Goodbye
Great Screams
Grim Reaper
Groups with Bird Names
Groups with Flower & Trees Names
Gypsies
Halloween
Halloween - Zacherle
Hangouts
Happy (& Not So Happy) Birthday
Happy Songs
Hearts
Heartaches
Heaven
Hey Songs
Hills (See Mountains)
House & Home
Hookers (See Second Oldest Profession)
Hot & Cold
Hotel
Indian
Inspirational
Instrumentals - Ventures

Instrumentals - Duane Eddy
Instrumentals - - Dick Dale
Jailbait
Jailbird Blues
Jungle Fever
Knocking
Laundromat
Lies
Light
Little Artists
Little Tunes
Lonely
Louie Louie
Love
Lovers
Love (Solo)
Magic
Mail Tunes
Mama's Advice
Mama & Papa
Man
Masturbation (See Love Solo)
Mercy Me
Midnight
Mine (Can You Dig It)
Money
Moon & Moonlight
Motorcycle
Mountains & Hills
Mr. & Mrs. (Ladie's First)
Night
No & Yes
Nobody
Nothing
Nonsense Syllables
Novelty Tunes
Novelty Tunes - Stan Freberg
Novelty Tunes - Ray Stevens
Novelty Tunes - Buchanon & Goodman
Numbers
Numbers - Thousands
Numbers - Millions & More
One Hit Wonders - Fabulous 50's
One Hit Wonders - Sensational 60's
One Hit Wonders - Swinging 70's
One Hit Wonders - Special Mention
Originals, Remakes, & Covers
Parks

Party Tunes
Patriotic
Pets (& Birds & Butterflies Are Free & Cats & Dogs & Horses)
Planes (See Trains & Boats &)
Poor (See Rich)
Private Eyes (Detectives too)
Psychedelic Sixties
Rain Songs (See Weather)
Rich & Poor
River
Rock & Roll
Royalty
Sad
Sailing
School
Sea Songs
Second Oldest Profession
Shoes
Sleep (See ZZZZZZ's)
Slow Jams
Soul
Spaced Out
Smoke (See Fire)
Snacks (See Candy or Food Fight)
Spelling Lesson
Star Songs
State of Mind
Stomp (See Dance Craze)
Summer Songs
Sun Songs (See Weather)
Surfin' Songs
Sweet Sixteen
Sweet Tooth & Snacks
Tears
Teen Idols (Girls)
Teen Idols (Guys)
Telephone #'s
The Day The Music Died
Time & Times
Time - Hours, Minutes, Seconds
Tonight
Trains & Boats & Planes
Tragedy (See Grim Reaper)
Two is Company
Three's A Crowd
Twist (See Dance Craze)
USA & Other Countries
Virgins

Walking
War & Peace
International Intrigue & 007
Weather & Wind & Rain Songs & Sun Songs
Wild Wild West
WILD!
Wind Songs (See Weather)
Wine Songs & Other Spirits
Woman
Yes (See No)
You Best Friend's Girl
Your Cheatin' Heart
ZZZZZZ's
A Very Brief History of Rock & Roll (In the Beginning, The Fifties & Beyond)
Scott Alan Murphy - The Soundtrack of My Life

Ain't (U Speek Gud, Now Ain't's in the Dictionary, Go Figure)

Ain't Goin' Down - Eric Clapton
Ain't Got No Home - Clarence "Frogman " Henry
Ain't No Mountain High Enough - Diana Ross / Marvin Gaye & Tammi Terrell
Ain't No Stopping Us Now - McFadden & Whitehead
Ain't No Sunshine - Bill Withers
Ain't No Way - Aretha Franklin
Ain't No Woman Like The One I Got - Four Tops
Ain't Nobody Home - Howard Tate
Ain't Nothin' You Can Do - Bobby Bland
Ain't Nothing Like The Real Thing - Marvin Gaye & Tammi Terrell
Ain't She Sweet - Beatles
Ain't Talkin' 'Bout Love - Van Halen
Ain't That A Shame - Fats Domino / Pat Boone
Ain't That Lovin' You Baby - Jimmy Reed
Ain't That Peculiar - Marvin Gaye
Ain't Too Proud to Beg - Temptations
Grits Ain't Groceries - Little Milton
He Ain't Heavy, He's My Brother - Hollies
I Ain't Got Nothin' - Temptations
I Ain't Got Time Anymore - Glass Bottle
I Ain't Got You - Billy Boy Arnold
I Ain't Superstituous - Howlin' Wolf
I Got It Bad & That Ain't Good - Duke Ellington
I Ain't Got Nobody to Love - Masqueraders
It Ain't Me (Who Are You Thinking Off) - Jimmy Rogers

It Ain't Me Babe - Turtles
Just a Gigolo / I Ain't Got Nobody - David Lee Roth
Rock & Roll Ain't Noise Pollution - AC / DC
TAin't Nothin' To Me - Coasters
Two Out of Three Ain't Bad - Meatloaf
We Ain't Got Nothing Yet - Blues Magoos
You Ain't Seen Nothin' Yet - BTO
Your Cash Ain't Nothin' But Trash - Huey Lewis & The News

Angels

Angel - Aerosmith
Angel - Angela Winbush
Angel - Aretha Franklin
Angel Baby - Rosie & The Originals
Angels Listened In - Crests
Angel of the Morning - Merilee Rush & The Turnabouts
Come On Little Angel - Belmonts
Devil or Angel - Clovers / Bobby Vee
Earth Angel - Penguins
Fools Rush In (Where Angels Fear to Tread) - Ricky Nelson
Heaven Must Be Missing an Angel - Tavares
Johnny Angel - Shelley Fabares
My Special Angel - Bobby Helms / Vogues
Next Door to an Angel - Neil Sedaka
Oh My Angel - Bertha Tillman / Kit Kats
Pretty Little Angel Eyes - Curtis Lee
Rockin' Little Angel - Ray Smith
Teen Angel - Mark Dinning
Undercover Angel - Alan O'Day
Honky Tonk Angel - Elvis Presley

& Devils

Dancing with Mr. D - Rolling Stones
Devil in His Heart - Donays
Devil or Angel - Clovers / Bobby Vee
Devil Woman - Cliff Richard
Devil Inside - INXS
Devil with a Blue Dress On - Mitch Ryder & The Detroit Wheels

Friend of the Devil - Grateful Dead
Race with the Devil - Gene Vincent
Running with the Devil - Van Halen
Sympathy for the Devil - Rolling Stones
(You're the) Devil in Disguise - Elvis Presley

Answer Songs (Sort of)

1000 Miles Away - Heartbeats ! Daddy's Home - Shep & The Limelights
It' My Party - Leslie Gore ! Judy's Turn to Cry - Leslie Gore
Flight 109 - Everly Brothers ! The Beverly Sisters - Flight 1203
My Guy - Mary Wells ! My Girl - Temptations
Space Oddity - David Bowie ! Major Tom - Peter Schilling
Wolverton Mountain - Claude King ! Girl from Wolverton Mountain
- Jo Ann Campbell
Work with Me Annie - Hank Ballard & The Midnighters ! Roll with Me
Henry - Etta James

At the Movies

Act Naturally - Beatles
Along Came Jones - Coasters
Horror Movies - Dickie Goodman
Popcorn - Hot Butter
Sad Movies (Make Me Cry) - Sue Thompson
Sitting in the Balcony - Eddie Cochran
Saturday Night at the Movies - Drifters
Wake Up Little Susie - Everly Brothers
Western Movies - Olympics

Baby Oh Baby

29 Ways (to My Babys Door) - Koko Taylor
(Sweet Sweet Baby) Since You've Been Gone - Aretha Franklin
(You're So Square) Baby I Don't Care - Elvis
Ain't That Loving You Baby - Jimmy Reed
Angel Baby - Rosie & The Originals
Baby Scratch My Back - Slim Harpo
Baby Baby Don't' Cry - Smokey Robinson & The Miracles
Baby Please Don't Go - Van Morrison

Baby I Love Your Way / Freebird (Free Baby) - Will to Power
Baby Don't Go - Sonny & Cher
Baby Oh Baby - Shells
Baby It's You - Shirelles
Baby Scratch My Back - Slim Harpo
Baby Baby Don't' Cry - Smokey Robinson & The Miracles
Baby Be Mine - Michael Jackson
Baby Come Back - Player
Baby It's Cold Outside - Ray Charles
B-A-B-Y - Carla Thomas
Baby Love - Supremes
Beach Baby - First Class
Baby I Love You - Aretha Franklin
Baby Let's Play House - Arthur Gunter
Baby Workout - Jackie Wilson
Baby Hold On - Eddie Money
Baby, What a Big Surprise - Chicago
Baby (You've Got What It Takes } - Brook Benton & Dinah Washington
Baby I'm Yours - Barbara Lewis
Baby Blue - Echos
Baby Don't Do It - Five Royales
Baby Now That I Found You - Foundations
Baby I Need Your Lovin' - Four Tops / Johnny Rivers
Baby Come to Me - James Ingram & Patti Austin
Baby Talk - Jan & Dean
Baby I Love Your Way - Peter Frampton
Baby Come Back - Player
Baby I'm for Real - Originals
Baby It's Cold Outside - Ray Charles
Baby What You Want Me to Do - Jimmy Reed
Baby Be Mine - Michael Jackson
Bang Bang (My Baby Shot Me Down) - Cher
Be Bop Baby - Ricky Nelson
Be My Baby - Ronettes
Bye Bye Baby - Commitments
Bye Bye Baby (Baby Goodbye) - Four Seasons
Can't Get Enough of Your Love Baby - Barry White
Come Back Baby - Ray Charles
Coney Island Baby - Excellents
Cradle of Love - Johnny Preston

Cry Baby - Garnet Mimms
Crying for My Baby - Little Junior Parker
Cry Baby Cry - Beatles
Cry Like a Baby - Box Tops
Double Shot (Of My Babys's Love) - Swinging Medallions
Don't Worry Baby - Beach Boys
Don't Say Nothin Bad (About My Baby) - Cookies
Everybody's Trying to Be My Baby - Carl Perkins / Beatles
Easy Baby - Magic Sam
Give Your Baby a Standing Ovation - Dells
Give It to Me Baby - Rick James
Goodbye Baby, Baby Goodbye - Solomon Burke
Goodbye Baby - Jack Scott
Happy Happy Birthday Baby - Tuneweavers
Hang On in There Baby - Johnny Bristol
Have Mercy Baby - Billy Ward & The Dominoes
Have You Seen Your Mother Baby Standing in the Shadows - Rolling Stones
Here Comes My Baby - Tremeloes
Hey Baby - Bruce Channel
How's Your Love Life Baby - Ted Taylor
I'm Gonna Love You Just a Little More Baby - Barry White
I Can't Quit You Baby - Otis Rush
Keep Your Hands Off Me Baby - Little Eva
Love My Baby - Little Junior's Blue Flames
Love to Love You Baby - Donna Summer
Make Me Your Baby - Barbara Lewis
Maybe Baby - Crickets
My Baby Left Me - Elvis
My Baby Must Be a Magician - Marvelettes
My Baby Loves Lovin' - White Plains
My Baby - Temptations
Need My Baby - Big Walter " Shakey " Horton
Nothings Too Good for My Baby - Stevie Wonder
Oh Baby What Would You Say - Hurricane Smith
Oh Me, Oh My (I'm a Fool for You Baby) - Aretha Franklin
Oh No Not My Baby - Maxine Brown
Ooh Baby Baby - Smokey Robinson & The Miracles / Linda Ronstadt
Ooh Wee Baby I Love You - Fred Hughes
Reconsider Baby - Lowell Fulson
Rock Me Baby - B.B. King

Rock Your Baby - George McCrae
Ruby Baby - Drifters / Dion
Run Baby Run (Back Into My Arms) - Newbeats
Since I Lost My Baby - Temptations
Since I Met You Baby - Ivory Joe Hunter
Stoop Down Baby - Chuck Willis
Sock it to Me Baby - Mitch Ryder & The Detroit Wheels
Sugar Baby Love - Rubettes
Take Good Care of My Baby - Bobby Vee
Talking About My Baby - Impressions
There Goes My Baby - Drifters
Too Busy Thinking About My Baby - Marvin Gaye
When Something is Wrong with My Baby - Sam & Dave
You're Having My Baby - Paul Anka
You Baby - Turtles
You Upset Me Baby - B.B. King
Yes Baby - Big Mama Thornton & Johnny Ace
You Don't Have to Be a Baby to Cry - Caravelles

Bad

40 Miles of Bad Road - Duane Eddy
Bad - Michael Jackson
Bad - U2
Bad Bad Leroy Brown - Jim Croce
Bad Boy - Jive Bombers
Bad to the Bone - George Thorogood & The Delaware Destroyers
Bad Time - Grand Funk
Bad Luck (Part I) - Harold Melvin & The Blue Notes
Bad Boys - Inner Circle (Theme from Cops)
Born Under a Bad Sign - Albert King
Bad Bad Whiskey - Amos Milburn
Bad Company - Bad Company
Bad to Me - Beatles / Billy Joe Royal & Dakotas
Bad Moon Rising - CCR
Call It Stormy Monday But Tuesday Is Just As Bad - T-Bone Walker
Don't Say Nothin' Bad (About My Baby) - Cookies
Good Lovin' Gone Bad - Bad Company
Hurt So Bad - Little Anthony & The Imperials / Linda Ronstadt
I'm Bad, I'm Nationwide - ZZ Top

I Feel So Bad - Chuck Willis / Elvis Presley
I Wanna Love Him So Bad - Jelly Beans
Need Your Love So Bad - Little Willie John
One Bad Apple - Osmonds
So Sad (To Watch Good Love Go Bad) - Everly Brothers
She's a Bad Mama Jama - Carl Carlton
Super Bad (Parts I & II) - James Brown
Two Out of Three Ain't Bad - Meatloaf
Why Does It Hurt So Bad - Whitney Houston

Baseball

Boys of Summer - Don Henley
Casey at the Bat - Jackie Gleason
Centerfield - John Fogarty
Glory Days - Bruce Springsteen
Mrs. Robinson - Simon & Garfunkel (Joe Dimaggio mention)

Beach & Boardwalk

Beach Baby - First Class
Cheap Sunglasses - ZZ Top
Love Letters in the Sand - Pat Boone
Sand in My Shoes - Drifters
Remember (Walkin' in the Sand) - Shangri Las
Under the Boardwalk - Drifters
Wildwood Days - Bobby Rydell

Bells

Bells of St. Mary's - Lee Andrews & The Hearts / Drifters
Church Bells May Ring - Willows / Diamonds
Hell's Bells - AC/DC
Lullaby of the Bells - The Deltaires
Mission Bells - Donnie Brooks
One Less Bell to Answer - Fifth Dimension
Rainy Day Bells - Globetrotters (As in Basketball Legends)
Ring My Bell - Anita Ward
The Three Bells - Browns
The Bells - Originals

Whispering Bells - Dell Vikings
Wedding Bell Blues - Fifth Dimension

Big Artists (It's Not About The Size)

Big Mama Thornton
The Big Bopper
Big Jay Neely
Big Brother & The Holding Co
Mr. Big

Big Tunes

A Big Hunk O'Love - Elvis Presley
In a Big Country - Big Country
Big Shot - Billy Joel
Big Bird - Eddie Floyd
Big Love - Fleetwood Mac
Big Girls Don't Cry - Four Seasons
Big Man in Town - Four Seasons
Big Boss Man - Jimmy Reed
Big Yellow Taxi - Joni Mitchell
Big Boy Pete - Olympics
Big Time Only - Peter Gabriel
Biggest Part of Me - Ambrosia
Bright Lights, Big City - Jimmy Reed
Give Him a Great Big Kiss - Shangri Las
Mr. Big Stuff - Jean Knight

Books

Book of Love - Monotones
Book of Dreams - Bruce Springsteen
Bookends - Simon & Garfunkel
Dear Diary - Moody Blues
Paperback Writer - Beatles
My Heart is an Open Book - Carl Dobkin's Jr.
My Back Pages - Bob Dylan
You Can't Judge a Book by the Cover - Stevie Wonder

Boys

A Girl Without a Boy - Annette
Bad Boy - Jive Bombers
Bad Boy / Having a Party - Luther Vandross
Bad Boys - Inner Circle (Theme from Cops)
Boy from New York City - Ad Libs / Manhattan Transfer
Big Boy Pete - Olympics
Boys of Summer - Don Henley
Cowboys to Girls - Intruders
Dirty White Boy - Foreigner
Dukes of Hazard (Good Old Boys) - Waylon Jennings
I Have a Boyfriend - Chiffons
Let's Hear It for the Boy - Deneice Williams
Little Boy Sad - Johnny Burnette
Lonely Boy - Paul Anka
Lonely Blue Boy - Conway Twitty
Loverboy - Billy Ocean
Mannish Boy - Muddy Waters
My One & Only Jimmy Boy - Girlfriends
My Boy Lollipop - Little Millie Small
Oh Boy - Crickets
Playboy - Marvellettes
Soldier Boy - Shirelles
Southern Country Boy - Carter Brothers
Space Cowboy - Steve Miller
Shoe Shine Boy - Eddie Kendricks
Smokin' in the Boy's Room - Brownsville Station
This Boy - Beatles
The All American Boy - Bill Parsons
That's the Way Boys Are - Leslie Gore
The Kind of Boy You Can't Forget - Raindrops
The Boys Are Back in Town - Thin Lizzy
Where the Boys Are - Connie Francis

Boy's Names

Abraham, Martin, & John - Dion
Ahab the Arab - Ray Stevens
You Can Call Me Al - Paul Simon

Bennie & The Jets - Elton John
Don't Mess With Bill - Marvelettes
Won't You Come Home Bill Bailey - Bobby Darin
My Girl Bill - Jim Stafford
Billy Don't Be A Hero - Bo Donaldson & The Heywoods
Bobby's Girl - Marcie Blane
Me & Bobby MaGee - Janis Joplin
Ode to Billy Joe - Bobby Gentry
Casey Jones - Grateful Dead
Charlie Brown - Coasters
Chuck E.'s in Love - Ricky Lee Jones
Mr. Custer - Larry Verne

Hey Jean, Hey Dean - Jean & Dean

Eddie My Love - Teen Queens
Eli's Coming - Three Dog Night

Do the Freddie - Freddie & The Dreamers / Chubby Checker
Freddie's Dead - Curtis Mayfield
Fernando - Abba

Wallflower (Roll with Me Henry) - Georgia Gibbs / Etta James
Harry The Hairy Ape - Ray Stevens

Hit the Road Jack - Ray Charles
Captain Jack - Billy Joel
Jumpin' Jack Flash - Rolling Stones
Jesse - Carly Simon
James Dean - Eagles
Don't Mess with Jim - Jim Croce
Jimmy Mack - Martha Reeves & The Vandellas
Quick Joey Small (Run Joey Run) - Kasenetz- Katz Singing
Orchestral Chorus
Killer Joe - Rocky Fellas
Run Joey Run - David Geddes
Hey Joe - Leaves / Jimi Hendrix
Big Bad John - Jimmy Dean
Johnny Angel - Shelley Fabares
Johnny B. Goode - Chuck Berry

Farmer John - Premiers
Hey Jude - Beatles
Kookie Kookie Lend Me Your Comb - Edd Byrnes & Connie Stevens
Hats Off to Larry - Del Shannon
Mr. Lee - Bobettes
Bad Bad Leroy Brown - Jim Croce
Levon - Elton John
Man Who Shot Liberty Valence - Gene Pitney
Louie Louie - Kingsmen
Luka - Suzanne Vega

Mack the Knife - Bobby Darin
Mickey's Monkey - Smokey Robinson & The Miracles

Norman - Sue Thompson

Tall Paul - Annette

Peter Gunn - Duane Eddy / Dick Dale
Big Boy Pete - Olympics

Rocky Raccoon - Beatles
Just Like Romeo & Juliet - Reflections

Stagger Lee - Lloyd Price
Boy Named Sue - Johnny Cash

Major Tom (Coming Home) - Peter Schilling
Ready Teddy - Little Richard
Tommy Can You Her Me - Who

Vincent - Don McLean

Willy & The Hand Jive - Johnny Otis Show
Little Willy - Sweet

CAR toons

There were more CARtoons in 1964 than any other year

409 - Beach Boys
Beep Beep - Playmates
Big Yellow Taxi - Joni Mitchell
Buick 59 - Medallions
Black & White T-Bird - Delicates
Brand New Cadillac - Vince Taylor
Bucket T - Ronnie & The Daytonas
Cadillac Man - Jesters
Cars - Gary Numan
Car Wash - Rose Royce
Car Hop - Exports
Cadillac Ranch - Bruce Springsteen
Come Back Maybelline - Mercy Dee
Chevy Van - Sammy Johns
Cruisin' - Hollywood Vines
Custom Machine - Bruce & Terry
Detroit City - Bobby Bare
Dead Man's Curve - Jan & Dean
Drag City - Jan & Dean
Drive - Cars
Drive My Car - Beatles
Drivin' Wheel - Little Junior Parker
Driver's Seat - Sniff N' The Tears
Every Woman I Know (is Crazy About an Automobile)
Expressway to Your Heart - Soul Survivors
Flat Tire - Del Vikings
Fun, Fun, Fun - Beach Boys (T-Bird)
Forty Miles of Bad Road - Duane Eddy
Four on the Floor - Shutdowns
Freeway of Love - Aretha Franklin
GTO - Ronnie & The Daytonas
Gasoline Alley - Rod Stewart
Gas Money - Jan & Arnie (before Jan & Dean)
Hey Little Cobra - Rip Chords
Hot Rod Lincoln - Johnny Bond / Commander Cody
Hotrod - Markeys
Highway Song - Blackfoot
Highway 61 Revisited - Bob Dylan / Edgar Winter
Highway to Hell - AC / DC
I Can't Drive 55 - Sammy Hagar

I Get Around - Beach Boys
Jenny Take a Ride - Mitch Ryder & The Detroit Wheels
Kentucky Rain - Elvis Presley
Key to the Highway - Little Walter
Keep on Truckin' (Part I) - Eddie Kendricks
Last Chance to Turn Around - Gene Pitney
L.A. Woman - Doors
Let's Get Lost on a Country Road - Kit Kats
Little Duece Coupe - Beach Boys
Little Old Lady from Pasadena - Jan & Dean
Little Red Corvette - Prince
Lord Mr. Ford - Jerry Reed
Maybelline - Chuck Berry
Mercedes Benz - Janis Joplin
Me & Bobby MaGee - Janis Joplin (written by Kris Kristofferson)
Mustang Sally - Wilson Pickett
Move Out Little Mustang - Rally Packs
Nadine (Is That You) - Chuck Berry
No Particular Place to Go - Chuck Berry
No Money Down - Chuck Berry
No Wheels - Chordettes
On the Road Again - Willie Nelson
Paradise by the Dashboard Light - Meatloaf
Pink Cadillac - Aretha Franklin
Pink Thunderbird - Gene Vincent
Plastic Jesus - Marrs Family
Rocket "88" - Jackie Brenston (Ike Turner's Kings of Rythmn)
Red Cadillac & a Black Mustache - Bob Luman
Radar Love - Golden Earring
Racing in the Street - Bruce Springsteen
Rockin' Down the Highway - Doobie Brothers
Roll On Down the Highway - Bachman Turner Overdrive (1975)
Roll Hot Rod Roll - Chuck McLolly
Route 66 Theme - Nelson Riddle & His Orchestra
Rumbleseat - John Cougar Mellencamp
Shutdown - Beach Boys
Seven Little Girls Sitting in the Back Seat - Paul Evans
Speedin' Medallions
Tell Laura I Love Her - Ray Petersen
Three Window Coupe - Ronnie & The Daytonas

The Anaheim, Azuza & Cucamonga Sewing Circle, Book Review, & Timing Association - Jan & Dean
Transfusion - Nervous Norvus
Vehicle - Ides of March
Ventura Highway - America (1972)
Why Don't You People Learn to Drive - Gene Vincent
Wreck on the Highway - Bill Haley & The Saddlemen
You Can't Catch Me - Chuck Berry

Candy

1,2,3 - Len Barry (with Dovells before he went solo)
Ballad of a Teenage Queen - Johnny Cash
Big Rock Candy Mountain - Burl Ives
Candy Girl - Four Seasons
Candy Man - Roy Orbison
Candy-O - Cars
Come On-a My House - Rosemary Clooney
I Want Candy - Strangeloves / Bow Wow Wow
Incense & Peppermints - Strawberry Alarm Clock
Lollipop - Chordettes
Lollipop Guild - The Wizard of Oz
My Boy Lollipop - Little Millie Small
Peppermint Twist - Joey Dee & the Starlighters
Rose & a Baby Ruth - George Hamilton IV
Sugar Sugar - Archies
Sunshine, Lollipops, & Rainbows - Leslie Gore

Cards

Deck of Cards - Wink Martindale
Queen of Hearts - Juice Newton
Two of Hearts - Stacy Q
The Joker - Steve Miller
The Gambler - Kenny Rogers

Catch Phrases

Groovin' - Rascals
Here Come Da Judge - Pigmeat Markham

Kind of a Drag - Buckinghams
Let It Out (Let It All Hang Out) - Hombres
Make My Day - T.G. Sheppard
Sock It to Me Baby - Mitch Ryder & The Detroit Wheels
Word Up - Cameo

Circus

Baby Elephant Walk - Henry Mancini / Bill Haley & His Comets
Cathy's Clown - Everly Brothers
Everybody Loves a Clown - Gary Lewis & The Playboys
Goodbye Cruel World - James Darren
Hurdy Gurdy Man - Donovan
Love Rollercoaster - Ohio Players
Monkey Time - Major Lance
Mickey's Monkey - Smokey Robinson & The Miracles
Roustabout - Elvis
Sideshow - Blue Magic
The Tears of a Clown - Smokey Robinson & The Miracles
Tiger - Fabian
The Lion Sleeps Tonight - Tokens / Kingston Trio / Robert john

Cities & Towns

Allentown - Billy Joel

Atlantic City - Bruce Springsteen

Dirty Water - Standells (Boston)

The Night Chicago Died - Paper Lace

L.A.Woman - Doors
I Love L.A. - Randy Newman
Coming into Los Angeles - Arlo Guthrie

All the Way from Memphis - Mott the Hoople
Memphis - Lonnie Mack / Johnny Rivers
Memphis - Bob Marley & The Wailers
Memphis Soul Stew - King Curtis

Walkin in Memphis - Marc Cohen

Nashville Cats - Lovin' Spoonful

City of New Orleans - Arlo Guthrie
New Orleans - Gary US Bonds
Way Down Yonder in New Orleans - Freddie Cannon
Witch Queen of New Orleans - Redbone
Walkin' to New Orleans - Fats Domino

Boy from New York City - Ad Libs / Manhattan Transfer
New York, New York - Frank Sinatra
New York's a Lonely Town - Tradewinds

Omaha - Moby Grape

Philadelphia Freedom - Elton John
Philadelphia - Neil Young
Streets of Philadelphia - Bruce Springsteen

San Antonio Rose - Patsy Cline

I Left My Heart in San Francisco - Tony Bennett
Lights - Journey (San Francisco)
Tallahasee Lassie - Freddie Cannon

Wildwood Days - Bobby Rydell (Wildwood, NJ)
Wildwood Boogie - Charlie Gracie
Wild About Wildwood - Treniers

234-5789 (Soulville, USA) - Wilson Pickett
Bright Lights, Big City - Jimmy Reed
Funkytown - Lipps Inc
Life in a Northern Town - Dream Academy
Margaritaville - Jimmy Buffet
My Hometown - Paul Anka
Suffragette City - David Bowie
Surf City - Jan & Dean
Village of Love - Nathaniel Mayer (1962)

Colors

Blue Monday - Fats Domino
Blue Velvet - Bobby Vinton
Blue On Blue - Bobby Vinton
Blue Bayou - Roy Orbison / Linda Ronstadt

Black is Black - Los Bravos
Back in Black - AC / DC
Black - Pearl jam
Black & White - Three Dog Night

Crimson & Clover - Tommy James & The Shondells

Green Tambourine - Lemon Pipers
Green Door - Jim Lowe
Green Eyed Lady - Sugarloaf
Green River - CCR
Green Onions - Booker T. & the MG's

Mellow Yellow - Donovan
Big Yellow Taxi - Joni Mitchell
Goodbye Yellow Brick Road - Elton John
Purple Raindrops - Stevie Wonder
Purple Rain - Prince

Red Roses for a Blue Lady - Bobby Vinton
Roses Are Red - Bobby Vinton
Red Rain - Peter Gabriel

White Christmas - Bing Crosby / Drifters
Nights in White Satin - Moody Blues

Choice of Colors - Impressions
True Colors - Cyndi Lauper

Cry

(If You Cry) True Love True Love - Drifters
Big Girls Don't Cry - Four Seasnos

Cry to Me - Betty Harris / Solomon Burke
Cry, Cry, Cry - Bobby Bland
Cry Like a Baby - Box Tops
Cry Baby Cry - Angels / Beatles
Cry Baby - Garnet Mimms
Crying for My Baby - Little Junior Parker
Crying - Don McLean
Fool to Cry - Rolling Stones
I Cried a Tear - LaVern Baker
I Don't Want to Cry - Chuck Jackson
I Wake Up Crying - Chuck Jackson
Little White Cloud That Cried - Johnny Ray
No Woman, No Cry - Bob Marley
You Don't Have to Be a Baby to Cry - Caravelles
You Don't Have to Cry - Crosby, Stills, & Nash

Dance

And We Danced - Hooters
Come Dancing - Kinks
Dance, Dance, Dance - Joey Dee & The Starlighters
Dance, Dance, Dance - Beach Boys
Dance, Dance, Dance (Yowsah) - Chic
Dance with Me - Drifters
Dance Across the Floor - Jimmy Horn (1978)
Dance to the Music - Sly & The Family Stone
Dancing in the Moonlight - King Harvest
Dancing Queen - ABBA
Dancing Machine - Jackson Five
Dancing with Mr. D - Rolling Stones
Dancin' Man - Q (1977)
Dance Little Sister - Terrance Trent D'Arby
Do You Love Me (Now that I Can Dance) - Contours
Do You Wanna Dance -Bobby Freeman / Del Shannon
Going to A Go Go - Smokey Robinson & The Miracles
Keep on Dancing - Gentrys
Keep On Dancin' - Gary's Gang
Land of 1000 Dances - Wilson Pickett / Cannibal & The Headhunters
Let The Little Girl Dance - Billy Bland
Let's Dance - Chris Montez

Let's Dance - David Bowie
Neutron Dance - Pointer Sisters
Safety Dance - Men Without Hats
Save the Last Dance for Me - Drifters
Tiny Dancer - Elton John
When You Dance - Turbans
Won't You Come Dance with Me - Commodores

Dance Craze

The 81 - Candy & The Kisses
Alley Cat - Bent Fabric / Bobby Rydell (with Words ?!?)
Barefootin' - Robert Parker
The Bop - Gene Vincent
Bongo Stomp - Little Joey & The Flips
Bristol Stomp - Dovells
Bugaloo - Tom & Jerrio
Conga - Gloria Estefan
Continental - Louis Jordan
Cool Jerk - Capitals
Crossfire - Orlons
Curly Shuffle - Back in the Saddle Band
Do the Bop - Danny & The Juniors (Never Released, became "At the Hop")
Discophonic Walk - Jerry Blavat
The Fish - Bobby Rydell
The Fly - Chubby Checker
Foot Stomping (Part I) - Flares
Do the Freddie - Freddie & The Dreamers / Chubby Checker
Hang on Sloopy - McCoys
Hitchhike - Marvin Gaye
Hokey Pokey - Traditional
Hucklebuck - Chubby Checker
Hully Gully (Baby) - Olympics
The Hustle - Van McCoy
The Jerk - Larks / Capitols
Let's Stomp - Bobby Comstock
Limbo Rock - Chubby Checker
Loop De Loop - Bobby Rydell
Mashed Potato - Dee Dee Sharp
Mashed Potatos with Gravy - Dee Dee Sharp

Monkee Time - Major Lance
Mess Around (Dance the) - Chubby Checker
Mickey's Monkey - Smokey Robinson & The Miracles
Madison Time - Ray Bryant (Calls by Eddie Morrison)
Popeye (The Hitchhiker) - Chubby Checker
Pop Pop Popeye - Sherrys
Pony Time - Chubby Checker
Rock Lobster - B-52's
Soul City Walkin' - Archie Bell & Drells
Shake - Sam Cooke / Otis Redding
Shout - Isley Brothers
Stroll - Diamonds
Surfin' Bird - Trashmen
The Swim - Bobby Freeman
Theme from New York, New York - Old Blue Eyes
Tighten Up - Archie Bell & Drells
The Twist * - Hank Ballard & The Midnighters / Chubby Checker
The Walk - Jimmy McCracklin
Walk Like an Egyptian - Bangles
Walk the Dinosaur - Was (Not Was)
Watusi - Vibrations
Wah Watusi - Orlons
Willie & Hand Jive - Johnny Otis
Y.M.C.A. - Village People

Dance Craze - **Special Mention** (for the DJs Who Are Sick of Them!)

Electric Slide - Marcia Griffiths (Actually a Reggae Tune)
New Electric Slide - Grand Master Flash & The Furious Five
Cha Cha Slide - Mr. C
Cotton Eyed Joe - Traditional
Macarena - Los Del Rio
Ride the Train - Quad City DJ's

Dance Craze -**Twist Tunes** *

Twist was written & performed by Hank Ballard & the Midnighters but did
not receive National recognition until it was recorded by Chubby Checker,
in fact, it was the only Rock & Roll song to hit #1 Twice Aug '60 & Nov '61

Bristol Twistin' Annie - Dovells
Dear Lady Twist - Gary US Bonds
Let's Twist Again - Chubby Checker
Slow Twistin' - Chubby Checker (with Dee Dee Sharp)
Teach Me to Twist - Chubby Checker & Bobby Rydell
Peppermint Twist - Joey Dee & The Starlighters
Perculator (Twist) - Billy Joe & The Checkmates
Soul Twist - King CurtisTwistin' Postman - Marvelettes
Twist Twist Senora - Gary US Bonds
Twistin' USA - Danny & The Juniors
Twistin' England - Danny & The Juniors
Twist & Shout - Isley Brothers
Twistin' Matilda - Jimmy Soul
Twistin By The Pool - Dire Straits
Twistin' The Night Away - Sam Cooke
Your Sister Can't Twist (But She Can Rock & Roll) - Elton John

Dance Craze - Cha Cha

Baby I Need Your Lovin' - Four Tops
Cherry Pink & Apple Blossom White - Prez Prado
Do The Cha Cha Cha - Bobby Rydell
Everybody Loves to Cha Cha Cha - Sam Cooke
I Don't Love You Anymore - Teddy Pendergrass
I Heard It Through the Grapevine - Marvin Gaye / Gladys Knight & The Pips
Now or Never - Elvis Presley
P.S. I Love You - Beatles
Susie Darlin' - Robin Luke
Um Um Um Um Um - Major Lance

Dance Craze - Stomp Songs

Bristol Stomp - Dovells
Can I Get A Witness - Marvin Gaye
Hey Little Girl - Syndicate of Sound
I Do - Marvellos / J. Geils Band
Let's Stomp - Bobby Comstock
Let's Stomp Again - Danny & The Juniors
Mine Exclusively - Olympics
Quicksand - Martha Reeves & The Vandellas

Rockin Robin - Bobby Day
South Street - Orlons

Dates

December 1963 (Oh What a Night) - Four Seasons
1984 - Van Halen
1999 - Prince & The Revolution
In the Year 2525 - Zager & Evans

Day

A Day in the Life - Beatles
A Hard Day's Night - Beatles
Another Day in Paradise - Phil Collins
Another Rainy Day in New York City - Chicago
All Day & All of the Night - Kinks
Any Day Now (My Wild Beautiful Bird) - Chuck Jackson
Babalu's Wedding Day - Eternals / Billy & The Essentials
Bang The Drum All Day - Todd Rundgren
Beggars Day - Crazy Horse
Dancing Days - Led Zeppelin
Day By Day - Hooters
Day Dreaming - Aretha Franklin
Daydream - Lovin' Spoonful
Daydream Believer - Monkees
Day Tripper - Beatles
Eight Days a Week - Beatles
Every Day I Have to Cry - Steve Alaimo
Every Day I Have the Blues - B.B. King
Forty Days - Ronnie Hawkins
Forty Days & Forty Nights - Muddy Waters
Glory Days - Bruce Springsteen
Here Comes That Rainy Day Feeling Again - Fortunes
Happy Days - Pratt & Mclain
I Think It's Going to Rain Today - Joe Cocker
I Saw Linda Yesterday - Dickey Lee
King for a Day - Thompson Twins
Let's Live for Today - Grass Roots
Lonely Days - Bee Gees

Lovely Day - Bill Withers
Nothing to Do But Today - Stephen Stills
Oh Happy Day - Edwin Hawkin's Singers
Our Day Will Come - Ruby & The Romantics
One Fine Day - Chiffons
Seven Lonely Days - Patsy Cline
School Days - Chuck Berry
Strange Days - Doors
That'll be the Day - Buddy Holly / Beatles / Linda Ronstadt
That Girl Belongs to Yesterday - Gene Pitney
Til the end of the Day - Kinks
Time Has Come Today - Chambers Brothers
Turn Down Day - The Cyrkle
Wildwood Days - Bobby Rydell
Yester-Me, Yester-You, Yester-Day - Stevie Wonder
Yesterday's Dreams - Four Tops
Yesterday - Beatles

Days of the Week

Blue Monday - Smiley Lewis / Fats Domino
Call It Stormy Monday, But Tuesday Is Just As Bad -T-Bone Walker
Come Monday - Jimmy Buffet
I Don't like Mondays - Boomtown Rats (Bob Geldof)
Manic Monday - Bangles
Monday Monday - Mamas & Papas
Stormy Monday Blues - Bobby Bland

Tuesday Afternoon - Moody Blues
Ruby Tuesday - Rolling Stones

Wednesday Morning 3am - Simon & Garfunkel
Wednesday - Royal Guardsmen

Thursday - Jim Croce
Thursdays Child - Earta Kitt
Sweet Thursday - Johnny Mathis

Friday on My Mind - Easy Beats
Thank God It's Friday - Love & Kisses

Livin' It Up (Friday Night) - Bell & James
Almost Saturday Night - Dave Edmunds
Saturday Night Fish Fry - Louis Jordan & His Tympany Five
Saturday Night - Bay City Rollers
Saturday Night's Alright for Fighting - Elton John
Saturday Night at the Movies - Drifters

Sunday Will Never Be the Same - Spanky & Our Gang
Groovin' (on a Sunday Afternoon) - Rascals
Sunday Kind of Love - Harptones
Sunday & Me - Jay & the Americans
Pleasant Valley Sunday - Monkees
I Met Him on a Sunday - Shirelles
Sunday Never Comes - CCR
Never on a Sunday (Traditional)
Sunday & Me - Jay & The Americans
Beautiful Sunday - Daniel Boone
Sunday Papers - Joe Jackson
Sunday Bloody Sunday - U2
Sugar on Sunday - Clique (produced by Tommy James & you can tell !)

Wild Weekend - Rockin' Rebels
Working for the Weekend - Loverboy
Eight Days a Week - Beatles
Six Nights a Week - Crests
Calendar Girl - Neil Sedaka

Dedicated Followers of Fashion

Black Slacks - Joe Bennett & The Sparkletones
Black Denim Trousers & Motorcycle Boots - Cheers
Blue Suede Shoes - Carl Perkins / Elvis Presley (See Covers & Remakes)
Bobby Sox to Stockings - Frankie Avalon
Dedicated Follower of Fashion - Kinks
Fashion - David Bowie
High Heel Sneakers - Tommy Tucker
Leather & Lace - Stevie Nicks
Pink Shoe Laces - Dodie Stevens
She's a Beauty - Tubes
Short Shorts - Royal Teens

Skin Tight - Ohio Players
These Boots Are Made for Walking - Nancy Sinatra
The Look - Roxette
Vogue - Madonna
White Sport Coat - Marty Robbins

Dreams

A Wonderful Dream - Majors
All I Have to Do is Dream - Everly Brothers
California Dreaming - Mamas & Papas
Don't Fall in Love with a Dreamer - Kenny Rogers & Kim Carnes
Dream Lover - Bobby Darin
Dream Girl - Stephen Bishop
Dreams - Fleetwood Mac
Dream Weaver - Gary Wright
Dreamboat Annie - Heart
Dreamin' - Johhny Burnette
Dreaming - Blondie
Gemini Dream - Moody Blues
Get Out of My Dreams & In to My Car - Billy Ocean
I Can Dream About You - Dan Hartman
Impossible Dream - Temptations
In Dreams - Roy Orbison
I Had Too Much to Dream Last Night - Electric Prunes
I Had a Dream - Johnny Taylor
I Like Dreaming - Kenny Nolan
Just a Dream - Jimmy Clanton
Like Dreamers Do - Beatles
Life is But a Dream - Harptones
Never Had a Dream Come True - Stevie Wonder
Oh What a Dream - Ruth Brown
Shattered Dreams - Johnny Hates Jazz
Sweet Dreams Are Made of This - Eurythmics
These Dreams - Heart
Yesterday's Dreams - Four Tops
Your Wildest Dreams - Moody Blues
Wildest Dreams - Asia

& Daydreams

Daydream - Lovin' Spoonful
Daydream Believer - Monkees
Day Dreaming - Aretha Franklin

Doctor, Doctor

Bad Case of Lovin' You - Robert Palmer
Doctor's Orders - Carol Douglas
Doctor My Eyes Jackson Brown
Dr. Feelgood - Aretha Franklin
Dr. Robert - Beatles
Jeremiah Peabody's Polyunsaturated, Quick Dissolving, Fast
Acting, Pleasant Tasting Green & Purple Pills - Ray Stevens
Rockin' Pneumonia & The Boogie Woogie Flu - Huey " Piano " Smith
Witch Doctor - David Seville

Drugs & Other States of Altered Perception

Big Shot - Billy Joel
Captain Jack - Billy Joel
Cocaine - Eric Clapton / J.J. Cale
Casey Jones - Grateful Dead
Coming into Los Angeles - Arlo Guthrie
Eight Miles High - Byrds
Incense & Peppermints - Strawberry Alarm Clock
Kicks - Paul Revere & the Raiders
Life in the Fast Lane - Eagles
Lucy in the Sky with Diamonds - Beatles
Mama Told Me Not to Come - Three Dog Night
Mothers Little Helper - Rolling Stones
One Toke Over the Line - Brewer & Shipley
Rainy Day Women #'s 12 & 35 - Bob Dylan
That Smell - Lynyrd Skynyrd

Eyes Have It!

Angel Eyes - Jeff Healy Band
Bette Davis Eyes - Kim Carnes

Brown Eyed Girl - Van Morrison
Close Your Eyes - Five Keys / Peaches & Herb
Don't It Make My Brown Eyes Blue - Crystal Gayle
Dry Your Eyes - Brenda & The Tabulations
Ebony Eyes - Everly Brothers / Bob Welch
Eye in the Sky - Alan Parson's Project
Green Eyed Lady - Sugarloaf
Heaven in Your Eyes - Loverboy
Hungry Eyes - Eric Carmen
I Only Have Eyes for You - Flamingos
Look in My Eyes - Chantels
Lost in Your Eyes - Debbie Gibson
Looking Through the Eyes of Love - Gene Pitney
My Eyes Adored You - Frankie Valli
Mystic Eyes - Them
Open My Eyes - Nazz
Pretty Little Angel Eyes - Curtis Lee
Private Eyes - Hall & Oates
Sad Eyes - Robert John
Suite: Judy Blue Eyes - Crosby, Stills, & Nash
Sexy Eyes - Dr. Hook
Somebody's Eyes - Karla Bonoff
Smoke Gets in Your Eyes - Platters
The Smile Has Left Your Eyes - Asia
The Night Has A Thousand Eyes - Bobby Vee
These Eyes - Guess Who
The Story in Your Eyes - Moody Blues
The Love Light Starts Shining Through His Eyes - Supremes
White Lies, Blue Eyes - Bullet

Family Affair

Cowsills (Bill, Bob, Barry, John, Susan, & Paul w Mom Barbara)
Everly Brothers (Don & Phil)
Isley Brothers (Ronald, Rudolph, & O'Kelly)
Jackson Five (Jackie, Tito, Jermaine, Marlon & Michael)
Neville Brothers (Arther, Charles, Aaron, & Cyril)
Partridge Family (Keith, Danny, Susan, & Shirley on Tambourine)
Pointer Sisters (Ruth, Anita, June & Bonnie)
Sister Sledge (Kathy, Debbie, Kim & Joni)

Sly & The Family Stone (Sly, Freddie, Rose, & Larry Graham)

Family Affair / Duos, Brothers, Sisters & Twins

Art & Dotty Todd
Ashford & Simpson (Nicholas Ashford & Valerie Simpson)
Billie & Lillie (Billy Ford & Lillie Bryant)
Dick & Dee Dee (Dick St. John & Dee Dee Sperling)
Gene & Debbie (Gene Thomas & Debbie Nevills)
Gene & Eunice (Gene Forrest & Eunice Levy)
Hall & Oates (Darryl Hall & John Oates)
Homer & Jethro (Homer Hanes & Jethro Burns)
James & Bobby Purify (James Purify & Robert Lee Dickey)
Johnnie & Joe (Johnnie Richardson & Joe Rivers)
Marvin & Johnny (Marvin Philips & Emory Perry, Jesse Belvin & Others)
Marvin Gaye & Tammy Terrell
Marvin Gaye & Kim Weston
Mickey & Silvia (Mickey Baker & Sylvia Robinson)
NinoTempo & April Stevens (Brother & Sister)
Paul & Paula (Ray Hildebrand & Jill Jackson)
Peaches & Herb (Francine Barker & Herb Fame)
Robert & Johnny (Robert Carr & Johnny Mitchell)
Simon & Garfunkel (Paul Simon & Art Garfunkel)
Skip & Flip (Gary Paxton & Clyde Battin)
Sonny & Cher (Salvatore " Sonny " Bono & Cherilyn LaPier)
Tom & Jerry (Simon & Garfunkel)
Tom & Jerry -O
Travis & Bob (Travis Pritchett & Bob Weaver)
Zager & Evans (Denny Zager & Richard Evans)

Everly Brothers (Don & Phil)
Isley Brothers (Ronald, Rudolph & O'Kelly)
Righteous Brothers (Bill Medley & Bobby Hatfield)
Walker Brothers (John Maus, Scott Engel, Gary Leeds)
Neville Brothers (Arther, Charles, Aaron, & Cyril)
Doobie Brothers (Tom Johnston, Pat Simmons, Michael McDonald, Jeff
"Skunk" Baxter, John Hartman, Keith Knudsen, & Tiran Porter)

Paris Sisters (Albeth, Priscilla & Sherrell)
Maguire Sisters (Christine, Dorothy, & Phyllis)

Pointer Sisters (Ruth, Anita, June & Bonnie)
Sister Sledge (Kathy, Debbie, Kim, & Joni)
Glimmer Twins (Mick Jagger & Keith Richards)
Thompson Twins (Tom Bailey, Allanah Currie & Joe Leeway)

Fire

Burning Down the House - Talking Heads
Fire - Bruce Springsteen / Pointer Sisters / Elmer Fudd
Fire - Crazy World of Arthur Brown
Fire - Ohio Players
Fire & Ice - Pat Benetar
Fire & Rain - James Taylor
I'm on Fire - Twight Twilley Band
Jump Into the Fire - Nilsson
Light My Fire - Doors
St. Elmo's Fire (A Man in Motion) - John Parr
We Didn't Start the Fire - Billy Joel

& Smoke

Hot Smoke & Sassafras - Bubble Puppy (1969)
Smoke from a Distant Fire - Sandford Townsend Band
Smoke Gets in Your Eyes - Platters
Smoke on the Water - Deep Purple
Smokey Part II - Cozy Cole
Smokey Places - Corsairs

Food Fight

Apple, Peaches, Pumpkin Pie - Jay & The Techniques
Bread & Butter - Newbeats
Chewy, Chewy, Chewy - Ohio Express
Cherry Pie - Marvin & Johnny / Skip & Flip
Give Peas a Chance - Murf the Surf (with apologies to John & Yoko)
Hot Pastrami - Dartells
Jam Up & Jelly Tight - Tommy Roe
Mashed Potato - Dee Dee Sharp
Mashed Potato with Gravy - Dee Dee Sharp
One Bad Apple - Osmonds

Polk Salad Annie - Jim Stafford
Peanut Butter - Marathons
Rice is Nice - Lemon Pipers
Sweet Pea - Tommy Roe
Smokey Joe's Cafe - Robins (Beans)
Sukayaki - Taste of Honey
Yummy, Yummy, Yummy - Ohio Express

Fools

A Fool in Love - Ike & Tina Turner
A Fool Such As I - Elvis
Chain of Fools - Aretha Franklin / Commitments
The Fool on the Hill - Beatles
Everybody Plays the Fool - Main Ingredient
Every Time Two Fools Collide - Kenny Rogers & Dottie West
Fool to Cry - Rolling Stones
Fools Rush In (Where Angels Fear to Tread) - Ricky Nelson
Foolin' - Def Leppard
Fooling Yourself (The Angry Young Man) - Styx
I Pity The Fool - Bobby Bland
I'm a Fool - Dino, Desi, & Billy
If You've Got to Make a Fool of Somebody - Johnny Ray
Oh Me Oh My (I'm a Fool for You Baby) - Aretha Franklin
Poor Little Fool - Ricky Nelson
She's a Fool - Leslie Gore
The Fool - Sanford Clark
What a Fool Believes - Doobie Brothers
What Kind of Fool Do You Think I Am - Tams / Bill Deal & The Rhondells
Why Do Fools Fall in Love - Frankie Lymon & The Teenagers
Won't Get Fooled Again - Who
You Found Yourself Another Fool - Elgins

& Foolish

My Foolish Heart - Paula Abdul
Foolish Beat - Debbie Gibson
Foolish Little Girl - Shirelles

Friends

Can We Still Be Friends - Todd Rundgren
Friends - Led Zeppelin
Friends - Elton John
Friends & Lovers - Gloria Loring & Carl Anderson
Me & My Friends - Red Hot Chili Peppers
My Best Friends Girl - Cars
That's What Friends Are For - Dionne Warwick & Friends
With A Little Help From My Firends - Beatles / Joe Cocker
Why Can't We Be Friends - War

Garage Rock (My favorite type of Rock, 'cause I can actually play it!)

Louie Louie - Kingsmen (The Ultimate Garage Rock Tune)
Dirty Water - Standells
Wild Thing - Troggs
Lies - Knickerbockers
I Live for the Sun - Sunrays
Hey Little Girl - Syndicate of Sound
The Rapper - Jaggerz
Mony Mony - Tommy James & Shondells
Jenny (867-5309) - Tommy Tutone
Just Like Me - Paul Revere & The Raiders

Getting Married

Babalu's Wedding Day - Eternals / Billy & The Essentials
Band of Gold - Freda Payne
Crying in the Chapel - Orioles / Elvis
Chapel of Love - Dixie Cups
Church Bells May Ring - Willows
Down the Aisle of Love - Quintones
Down the Aisle - Patti LaBelle & The Blue Bells
I Wish We Were Married - Ronnie & Hilites
I'm Gonna Get Married - Lloyd Price
I'm Walking Behind You - Eddie Fisher
The Wedding Song (There is Love) - Peter, Paul, & Mary
Third Finger Left Hand - Martha Reeves & The Vandellas
To the Aisle - Five Satins

Wedding Bell Blues - Fifth Dimension
When We Get Married - Dreamlovers
White Wedding I & II - Billy Idol
Worst That Could Happen - Brooklyn Bridge

Girl Groups

Ad Libs
Angels
Blossoms
Bobettes
Chantels
Chiffons
Crystals
Cookies
Cascades
Cookie & the Cupcakes
Deltairs
Dixie Cups
Exciters
Girlfriends
Jaynetts
Jelly Beans
Kathy Young & The Innocents
Murmaids
Orlons
Paris Sisters
Patti LaBelle & the Blue Belles
Poni Tails
Quintones
Raindrops
Reparata & the Delrons
Ronettes
Rosie & The Originals
Sensations
Shangri Las
Shirelles
Starlets
Teen Queens
Toys

Velvelettes
Vernon Girls

Girl Groups - Motown Division

Martha Reeves & The Vandellas
Marvelettes
Supremes (Primettes)

Girls

(Girls, Girls, Girls) Were Made to Love - Eddie Hodges
A Girl Without a Boy - Annette
A Girl Like You - Rascals
American Girl - Tom Petty & The Heartbreakers
Ask Any Girl - Supremes
Big Girls Don't Cry - Four Seasons
Boogie Woogie Country Girl - Big Joe Turner
Brandy (You're A Fine Girl) - Looking Glass
Brown Eyed Girl - Van Morrison
Bobby's Girl - Marcie Blane
Candy Girl - Four Seasons
Calendar Girl - Neil Sedaka
California Girls - Beach Boys / David Lee Roth
Catholic School Girls Rule - Red Hot Chili Peppers
China Girl - David Bowie
Cowboys to Girls - Intruders
Dream Girl - Steven Bishop
Diamond Girl - Seals & Crofts
Fat Bottomed Girls - Queen
Foolish Little Girl - Shirelles
For Me & My Girl - Nilsson
Girl Watcher - O'Kaysions
Girl of My Dreams - Bram Tchaikovsky
Girl of My Best Friend - Ral Donner & The Starfires
Girl (Why You Wanna make Me Blue) - Temptations
Girlfriend - Pebbles
Good Girls Don't - Knack
Girl - Beatles
Girls Talk - Dave Edmunds

Girls - Dwight Twilley
Girl Come Running - Four Seasons
Girl Can't Help It - Journey
Hot Girls in Love - Loverboy
Hello Little Girl - Beatles
Here Comes the Girl - Tom Petty & The Heartbreakers
Hey Girl - Freddie Scott
Hey Little Girl - Major Lance
Hey Little Girl - Dee Clark
Hey Girl Don't Bother Me - Tams
Hey There Lonely Girl - Eddie Holman
I Want You to Be My Girl - Frankie Lymon & The Teenagers
Island Girl - Elton John
Image of a Girl - Safaris
Jesse's Girl - Rick Springfield
Let the Little Girl Dance - Billy Bland
Little Girl of Mine - Cleftones
Little Girl - Syndicate of Sound
Lovergirl - Teena Marie
Material Girl - Madonna
Mixed Up, Shook Up Girl - Patti & The Emblems
My Girl Sloopy - Vibrations
My Girl - Temptations
My Girl Josephine - Fats Domino
My Best Friend's Girl - Cars
Oh Girl - Chi Lites
Pretty Little Girl - Monarchs
Pretty Girls Everywhere - Eugene Church & The Fellows
Quicksilver Girl - Steve Miller Band
Reet Petite (Finest Girl You Ever Want to Meet) - Jackie Wilson
Rich Girl - Hall & Oates
Sad Girl - Jay Wiggins / Intruders / Hank Ballard & The Midnighters
San Francisco Girls (Return of the Native) - Fever Tree
See That Girl - Righteous Brothers
She's My Girl - Turtles
Sunshine Girl - Parade
Surfer Girl - Beach Boys
The Girl from Yesterday - Eagles
The Little Girl i Once Knew - Beach Boys
That's What Girls Are Made For - Spinners

The Girl's Alright With Me - Temptations
This Girl is Mine - Michael Jackson & Paul McCartney
This Girl is a Woman Now - Gary Pluckett & The Union Gap
The Girl Belongs to Yeaterday - Gene Pitney
The Girl Can't Help It - Little Richard
This Little Girl - Gary US Bonds
Uptown Girl - Billy Joel
Use Ta Be My Girl - O'Jays
Working My Way Back to You / Forgive Me Girl - Spinners
When She Was My Girl - Four Tops
When My Little Girl is Smiling - Drifters
Waiting for a Girl like You - Foreigner
Young Girl - Gary Pluckett & The Union Gap

Girl's Names

Arizona - Mark Lindsay
Angie - Rolling Stones
Amanda - Boston
Ariel - Dean Freidman (1977)
Abigail Beecher - Freddie Cannon
Alison - Elvis Costello
Work with Me Annie - Hank Ballard & The Midnighters
Annie Had a Baby - Hank Ballard & The Midnighters
Amie - Pure Prairie League

Barbara Ann - Regents / Beach Boys (with Dean Torrence)
Bernadette - Four Tops
Brandy - Looking Glass
Bertha Lou - Clint Miller
Betty Lou's Got a New Pair of Shoes - Bobby Freeman
Billy Jean - Michael Jackson
Bette Davis Eyes - Kim Carnes
Beth - Kiss
My Bonnie - Beatles

Cathy's Clown - Everly Brothers
Close to Cathy - Mike Clifford (1962)
Lawdy Miss Clawdy - Lloyd Price
Caldonia - Louis Jordan

Candida - Tony Orlando & Dawn
Connie O - Four Seasons
Carrie-Anne - Hollies
Cecilia - Simon & Garfunkel
Cindy Oh Cindy - Vince Martin & The Tarriers
Candy-O - Cars
Oh Carol - Neil Sedaka
Candy's Room - Bruce Springsteen
Clementine - Bobby Darin
Claudette - Roy Orbison / Everly Brothers
Corinne Corinna - Joe Turner
Carol - Chuck Berry
Cindy's Birthday - Johnny Crawford
Sweet Caroline - Neil Diamond

Diane - Bachelors
Desiree - Charts
Donna - Richie Valens
Donna the Prima Donna - Dion
Little Diane - Dion
Diana - Paul Anka
Denise - Randy & Rainbows
Dawn (Go Away) - Four Seasons

Elenore - Turtles
Come On Eileen - Dexy's Midnight Runners
Elenore Rigby - Beatles

Annie's Aunt Fannie - Hank Ballard & The Midnighters
Fannie Mae - Buster Brown
Florence - Paragons

Gloria - Them (Van Morrison) / Shadows of Knight / Doors
Georgie Girl - Seekers
Georgia On My Mind - Ray Charles

Heather Honey - Tommy Roe
Hooray for Hazel - Tommy Roe

Goodnight Irene - Weavers

Jenny Jenny - Little Richard
My Girl Josephine - Fats Domino
Jennifer Juniper - Donovan
(Just Like) Romeo & Juliet - Reflections
Jenny Take a Ride - Mitch Ryder & The Detroit Wheels
Jenny Lee - Jan & Arnie
Jamie - Eddie Holland
Dammit Janet - Barry Bostwick (Rocky Horror Picture Show)
Julia - Beatles
Ride on Josephine - George Thorogood & The Delaware Destroyers
Jeanie Jeanie Jeanie - Eddie Cochran
Little Jeannie - Elton John
Hey Jean, Hey Dean - Jean & Dean
Jenny (867-5309) - Tommy Tutone
Judy in Disguise - John Fred & His Playboy Band
Joanna - Kool & The Gang
Suite: Judy Blue Eyes - CSN
Sweet Jane - Velvet Underground

Ko Ko Mo (I Love You So) - Gene & Eunice

Ah Leah - Donnie Iris
Leah - Roy Orbison
Lucille - Little Richard
Lucille - Kenny Rogers
I'm Not Lisa - Jesse Colter (1975)
Lucy in the Sky with Diamonds - Beatles
Layla - Derek & The Dominoes / Eric Clapton (Acoustic)
Linda Lu - Ray Sharpe
Twistin' with Linda - Isley Brothers
Lola - Kinks
Darling Lorraine - Knockouts
Get Back (Loretta) - Beatles
Honalulu Lulu - Jan & Dean
I Saw Linda Yesterday - Dickie Lee
Liza Jane - Kit Kats
Tell Laura I Love Her - Ray Petersen

Marylou - Ronnie Hawkins
Maybelline - Chuck Berry

Hello Marylou - Ricky Nelson
Marlena - Four Seasons
Along Comes Mary - Association
Midnight Mary - Joe Powers
Sweet Mary - Wadsworth Mansion (1970)
Wind Cries Mary - Jimi Hendrix
My Maria - B.W.Stevenson (1973)
Good Golly Miss Molly - Little Richard
Devil with the Blue Dress On / Good Golly Miss Molly - Mitch Rider
& The Detroit Wheels
Michelle - Beatles
Martha My Dear - Beatles
Proud Mary - CCR / Ike & Tina Turner
Mony Mony - Tommy James & The Shondells / Billy Idol
Melissa - Allman Brothers
Lady Madonna - Beatles
(Marie's the Name) Of His Latest Flame - Elvis
C'mon Marianne - Four Seasons
Mandy - Barry Manilow
Maggie Mae - Rod Stewart
Maggie's Farm - Bob Dylan
Take a Letter Maria - R.B. Greaves
Crosseyed Mary - Jethro Tull
Mona Lisa - Nat King Cole

Nadine (Is That You?) - Chuck Berry
Nikita - Elton John

Peggy Sue - Buddy Holly
Peggy Sue Got Married - Buddy Holly
Dear Prudence - Beatles
Hey Paula - Paul & Paula
Peg - Steely Dan
Patricia - Prez Prado

Ruby Baby - Drifters / Dion / Beatles
Help Me Rhonda - Beach Boys
Roberta - Reverend Billy C. Wirtz
Rhiannon - Fleetwood Mac
Ronnie - Four Seasons

Roxanne - Police
Lovely Rita - Beatles
Love Grows (Where My Rosemary Goes) - Edison Lighthouse
Ruby, Don't Take Your Love to Town - Kenny Rogers
Cracklin' Rosie - Neil Diamond
Rosalita - Bruce Springsteen
Rosanna - Toto
Walk Away Renee - Left Banke / Four Tops

Sandy - Larry Hall
Sandy - Dion
Sherry - Four Seasons
Sheila - Tommy Roe
Lay Down Sally - Eric Clapton
My Sharona - Knack
Sara - Fleetwood Mac
Sara Smile - Hall & Oates
Sally's Sayin' Something - Billy Harner
Long Tall Sally - Little Richard
My Girl Sloopy -_Vibrations
Hang on Sloopy - McCoys
Mustang Sally - Wilson Pickett
Sexy Sadie - Beatles
Stormy - Classics IV
Sunny - Bobby Hebb
Sneakin' Sally Through the Alley - Robert Palmer

Tammy - Debbie Reynolds
Tracy - Cufflinks

Valerie - Monkees
Venus - Frankie Avalon
Venus - Shocking Blue

Windy - Association
Wendy - Beach Boys

Girl's Names - Susie Songs

Runaround Sue - Dion

Susie Darlin' - Robin Luke
Sweet Susie - Johnny Burnette
Susie Q - Dale Hawkins / CCR
Sweet Sue, Just You - Big Joe Turner / Bill Haley & His Comets
Tra La La La Suzy - Jan & Dean
Wake Up Little Susie - Everly Brothers
That's My Little Suzie - Richie Valens
Lonesome Susie - Band
Little Susie - Michael Jackson
Susie Cincinnati - Beach Boys
Susan - Buckinghams
Where's the Playground Susie - Glen Campbell
Boy Named Sue - Johnny Cash

Girl's Names - Nicknames

Be-Bop-A-Lula - Gene Vincent
Bony Maronie - Larry williams
Dizzy Miss Lizzie - Larry Williams
Gidget - James Darren
Jellie Bellie Nellie - Larry Williams
Kiddio - Brook Benton
Little Latin Lupe Lu - Righteous Brothers
Reet Petite (Finest Girl You Ever Want to Meet) - Jackie Wilson
Short Fat Fannie - Larry Williams
Sweet Pea - Tommy Roe

Name Game - Shirley Ellis

Good

A Rockin' Good Way (To Mess Around & Fall in Love) - Dinah
Washington & Brook Benton
Be Good To Me - Tina Turner
Devil with a Blue Dress On / Good Golly Miss Molly - Mitch Ryder &
The Detroit Wheels
Dr. Feelgood - Aretha Franklin
Dukes of Hazard Theme (Good Old Boys) - Waylon Jennings
Everybody Knows About My Good Thing - Johnny Taylor
Feelin' Good - Little Junior & The Blue Flames

Feel So Good - Shirley & Lee / Bunny Sigler / Johnny Preston
Feels So Good (I Want to Boogie) - Magic Sam
Get On the Good Foot (Part I) - James Brown
Gimme Gimme Good Lovin' - Crazy Elephant
Gonna Have a Funky Good Time - James Brown
Good Girls Don't - Knack
Good Good Feeling - War
Good Golly Miss Molly - Little Richard
Good Lovin' Gone Bad - Bad Company
Good Lovin' - Clovers / Rascals
Good Luck Charm - Elvis
Good Man, Good Woman - Bonnie Raitt & Delbert McClinton
Good Morning, Good Morning - Beatles
Good Night - Beatles
Good Old Rock & Roll - Cat Mother & The All Night Newsboys
Good Rockin' Tonight - Elvis
Good Times Roll - Cars
Good Thing - Paul Revere & The Raiders
Good Timin' - Jimmy Jones
Good Times - Chic
Goody Two Shoes - Adam Ant
Good Vibrations - Beach Boys
Good Vibrations - Marky Mark & The Funky Bunch
Good Morning Little School Girl - John Lee Hooker / Eric Clapton / Others
I Got You (I Feel Good) - James Brown
I'll Be Good to You - Brothers Johnson
I'm Into Something Good - Earl Jean
Life's Been Good - Joe Walsh
Let The Good Times Roll - Shirley & Lee
Nothings Too Good for My Baby - Stevie Wonder
Only the Good Die Young - Billy Joel
So Sad (To Watch Good Love Go Bad) - Everly Brothers
Sometimes Good Guys Don't Wear White - Standells
Tell Me Something Good - Rufus
Think of the Good Times - Jay & The Americans
Take Good Care of My Baby - Bobby Vee
You'll Lose a Good Thing - Barbara Lynn
You're No Good - Bette Everett
You're No Good - Linda Ronstadt
Your Good Thing is About to End - Mabel John

Goodbye

Bye Bye Baby (Baby Goodbye) - Four Seasons
Goodbye Baby - Jack Scott
Goodbye Baby (Baby Goodbye) - Solomon Burke
Goodbye Cruel World - James Darren
Goodbye Yellow Brick Road - Elton John
Hello, Goodbye - Beatles
Kiss & Say Goodbye - Manhattans
Lovers Never Say Goodbye - Flamingos
Na Na Hey Hey Kiss Him Goodbye - Steam
Neither One of Us (Wants to be the First to Say Goodbye) - Gladys Knight
& The Pips
Never Can Say Goodbye - Gloria Gaynor
Never Can Say Goodbye - Jackson Five
Say Goodbye to Hollywood - Billy Joel
Then you Can Tell Him Goodbye - Casinos
We'll Never Have to Say Goodbye Again - England Dan & John Ford Coley

Great Screams

I Feel Good - James Brown
Sugaree - Rusty York
I Put a Spell on You - Screaming Jay Hawkins

Grim Reaper

Death of An Angel - Donald Woods & the Bel Aires
Don't Fear the Reaper - Blue Oyster Cult
Earth Angel - Penguins
Endless Sleep - Jody Reynolds
Flight 109 - Everly Brothers
I Want My Baby Back - Jimmy Cross
Last Kiss - J. Frank Wilson & Cavaliers
Laurie (Strange Things Happen in this World) - Dickie Lee
Leader of the Pack - Shangri Las
Leader of the Laundromat - Detergents
Moody River - Pat Boone
Ode to Billy Joe - Bobby Gentry
Teen Angel - Mark Dinning

Tell Laura I Love Her - Ray Petersen
The Night The Lights Went Out in Georgia - Vicki Lawrence
Tragedy - Thomas Wayne & The DeLons
Let's Think About Livin' - Bob Luman

Groups with Bird Names

Byrds
Cardinals
Crows
Eagles
Flamingos
Flock of Seagulls
Larks
Partridge Family
Penguins
Robins

Groups with Flower & Tree Names

Carnations
Clovers
Gladiolas
Grass Roots
Hemlocks
Hollies
Leaves
Magnolias
Seeds
Willows

Gypsies

Gypsy - Fleetwood Mac
Gypsy Man - War
Gypsys, Tramps & Theives - Cher
Gypsy Wedding - Moby Grape
Gypsy Woman - Impressions / Four Seasons
Gypsy Woman (She's Homeless) - Crystal Waters
Has Anyone Seen My Gypsy Rose - Tony Orlando & Dawn

The Gypsy Cried - Lou Christie

Halloween

Addam's Family Theme - Vic Mizzy
All You Zombies - Hooters
Attack of the Killer Tomatoes - Lewis Lee
Black Magic Woman - Fleetwood Mac / Santana
Do You Believe in Magic - Lovin' Spoonful
Dead Man's Stroll - Revels
Devil Woman - Cliff Richard
Evil - Howlin' Wolf
Evil Woman - ELO
Frankenstein - Edgar Winter Group
Ghostbusters - Ray Parker Jr
Haunted House - Jumpin' Gene Simmons
Horror Movies - Dickie Goodman
I Put a Spell on You - Screaming Jay Hawkins
I Want My Baby Back - Jimmy Cross
Maneater - Hall & Oates
Martian Hop - Ran Dells
Monster Mash - Bobby "Boris" Pickett & The Crypt Kicker Five
Mummy's Ball - Verdicts
One Way or Another - Blondie
Purple People Eater - Shep Wooley
Peek A Boo - Cadillacs
Spooky - Classics IV
The Mummy - Bobby MacFadden & Dor
Thriller - Michael Jackson
The Blob - Five Blobs
Twilight Zone - Neil Norman & His Cosmic Orchestra
Welcome to My Nightmare - Alice Cooper
Werewolves of London - Warren Zevon
Witchcraft - Frank Sinatra
Witch Queen of New Orleans - Redbone
Witch Docter - David Seville
Witchy Woman - Eagles
Season of the Witch - Donovan
Zombie Jamboree - Kingston Trio

Halloween - Zacherle (The Cool Ghoul aka Roland or Zacherle)

John Zacherle did a Classic Horror Movie Show on WCAU TV in Philly
as Roland, & later in New York City as Zacherle as a deathly character
in undertakers garb. He would cut into the Classic Horror Movies
he played to a scene with him mixing a potion, hiding behind a rock,
or some other nonsense. Due to the low budget, there were other
characters on the show, you never saw. Igor, his assistant & his wife
"My Dear" (really a head of cabbage). He played all of the classic Horror
films, Frankenstein, Dracula, Wolfman, et al He had a real cult following.
It's where I got my love of the Classic Horror Flicks. As a kid I begged
to stay up to watch him. I was among his legion of fans. He was even
featured in one of my favorite mags Forrest Ackerman's Famous Monsters
of Filmland! ....Goodnight "My Dear" Whatever You Are!!!!

Dinner with Drac
Dinner with Drac II (with Toned Down Lyrics)
Igor
Hurry Bury Baby
Halloween Hootenanny
I'm the Ghoul from Wolverton Mountain
Let's Twist Again (Mummy Time is Here)
Limb from Limbo Rock
Pistol Stomp
Monster Mash (Remake)
Surfboard 1-0-9
Monster Mash
Sinister Purpose (with Southern Culture on the Skids)

Hangouts

I Like It Like Yhat - Chris Kenner
Love Shack - B-52's
Saturday Night Fish Fry - Louis Jordan
Sugar Shack - Jimmy Gilmer & The Fireballs

Happy (& Not So Happy) Birthday Songs

Birthday - Beatles
Bithday Party - Pixies Three

Cindy's Birthday - Johnny Crawford
Happy Birthday to You - Eddy Howard & His Orchestra
Happy Birthday - Stevie Wonder
Happy Birthday - Weird Al Yankovic
Happy Birthday - Bugs Bunny, Daffy Duck, Taz & The Gang
Happy Birthday Mr. President - Marilyn Monroe
Happy Birthday Elvis - Loudon Wainwright III
Happy Birthday Blues - Kathy Young & The Innocents
Happy Birthday Sweet Sixteen - Neil Sedaka
Happy Happy Birthday Baby - Tuneweavers
It's My Party - Leslie Gore
Laurie (Strange Things Happen in this World) - Dickie Lee
Sixteen Candles - Crests

Happy Songs

Don't Worry, Be Happy - Bobby McFerrin
I'm a Happy Man - Jive Five
Happiness is a Warm Gun - Beatles
Happy Organ - Dave "Baby" Cortez
Happy Song (Dum Dum) - Otis Redding
Happy Trails to You - Roy Rogers & Dale Evans
Happy Days - Pratt & McLean
Oh How Happy - Shades of Blue
Oh Happy Day - Edwin Hawkins Singers
Sha La La (Make Me Happy) - Al Green

Hearts

Be Still My Beating Heart - Sting
Burning Heart - Survivor
Cold Hearted - Paula Abdul
Devil in His Heart - Donays
Don't Go Breaking My Heart - Elton John & Kiki Dee
Don't Be Cruel (To a Heart That's True) - Elvis
Every Beat of My Heart - Taylor Dayne
Every Beat of My Heart - PipsHeartbeat - Buddy Holly
Expressway to Your Heart - Soul Survivors
Fortress Around Your Heart - Sting
Harden My Heart - Quarterflash

He Will Break Your Heart - Jerry Butler
Heart - Jordan Brothers
Heart of Glass - Blondie
Heart of Stone - Rolling Stones
Heart of Rock & Roll - Huey Lewis & The News
Heartbreak Hotel - Elvis
Hearts - Marty Balin
Hearts of Stone - Charms / Fontaine Sisters
Heart & Soul - Cleftones
Heart Full of Soul - Yardbirds
Heartbeat It's a Lovebeat - DeFranco Family
Hotrod Hearts - Robbie Dupree
How Can You Mend a Broken Heart - Bee Gees
Hungry Heart - Bruce Springsteen
I'm Gonna Let My Heart Do The Walking - Supremes
Listen to Her Heart - Tom Petty & The Heartbreakers
Listen to Your Heart - Roxette
Love is Like An Itching in My Heart - Supremes
My Heart is an Open Book - Carl Dobkins Jr.
Owner of a Lonely Heart - Yes
Only Love Can Break a Heart - Gene Pitney
Open the Door to Your Heart - Darrel Banks
Pain in My Heart - Otis Redding
Piece of My Heart - Irma Franklin / Big Brother & The Holding Co
Put a Little Love in Your Heart - Jackie DeShannon
Queen of Hearts - Juice Newton
Rainin' in My Heart - Slim Harpo
Save Your Heart for Me - Gary Lewis & The Playboys
Sgt Pepper's Lonely Hearts Club Band - Beatles
She's a Heartbreaker - Gene Pitney
Steal Your Heart Away - Bonnie Raitt
Stop Draggin' My Heart Around - Stevie Nicks
Straight from the Heart - Bryan Adams
Take These Chains from My Heart - Ray Charles
Tell It to My Heart - Taylor Dayne
Two of Hearts - Stacy Q
Two Hearts - Stephanie Mills & Teddy Pendrgras
The Heart of the Matter - Don Henley
This Old Heart of Mine - Isley Brothers
Total Eclipse of the Heart - Bonnie Tyler

Unchain My Heart - Ray Charles
What Becomes of the Brokenhearted - Jimmy Ruffin
You Gotta Have Love in Your Heart - Four Tops & Supremes
Young Hearts Run Free - Candi Staton
Your in My Heart (Final Acclaim) - Rod Stewart
Your Heart Belongs to Me - Supremes

Heartaches

Half Heaven, Half Heartache - Gene Pitney
Heartaches - Marcels
Heartaches By The Numbers - Guy Mitchell / Connie Francis
How the Heartaches Are Made - Baby Washington
It's a Heartache - Bonnie Tyler
Nothing But Heartaches - Supremes
Nothing But a Heartache - Flirtations
That's When Your Heartaches Begin - Elvis Presley

Heaven

Half Heaven, Half Heartache - Gene Pitney
Heaven on Earth - Platters
Heaven Help Us All - Stevie Wonder
Heavan Must Have Sent You - Elgins / Bonnie Pointer
Heaven - Bryan Adams
Heaven Must Be Missing an Angel - Tavares
Heaven Knows - Commodores
Jackie Wilson Said (I'm in Heaven When You Smile) - Van Morrison
Knocking on Heaven's Door - Bob Dylan
Rock & Roll Heaven - Righteous Brothers
Stairway to Heaven - Neil Sedaka (Also song by Led Zeppelin)
Teenage Heaven - Johnny Cymbal
Too Much Heaven - Bee Gees

Hey Songs

(Hey) Little Girl - Syndicate of Sound
Hey Baby - Bruce Channel
Hey ET - Buchanon & Goodman
Hey Girl Don't Bother Me - Tams

Hey Hey - Eric Clapton
Hey Hey What Can I Do - Led Zeppelin
Hey Jean, Hey Dean - Jean & Dean
Hey Joe - Leaves / Jimi Hendrix
Hey Jude - Beatles
Hey Lawdy Mama - Steppenwolf
Hey Little Girl - Dee Clark
Hey Little Girl - Major Lance
Hey Little School Girl - Tom & Jerry (Simon & Garfunkel)
Hey Love - Delfonics
Hey Love - Stevie Wonder
Hey There Lonely Girl - Eddie Holman
Hey Tonight - CCR
Hey Western Union Man - Jerry Butler

House

Animal House - Stephan Bishop (Animal House Sound Track)
Burning Down the House - Talking Heads
C'mon a My House - Rosemary Clooney
House of the Rising Sun - Animals
Something Strange is Going On in My House - Ted Taylor
The House That Jack Built - Aretha Franklin
This Old House - Rosemary Clooney

& Home

A House is Not a Home - Luther Vandross
Ain't Got No Home - Clarence "Frogman" Henry
Ain't Nobody Home - Howard Tate
Bring It on Home - Sonny Boy Williamson
Bring It on Home to Me - Sam Cooke / Animals
Call Me (Come Back Home) - Al Green
Can't Find My Way Home - Blind Faith
Close to Home - Grand Funk Railroad
Comin' Home - Delaney & Bonnie & Friends
Daddy's Home - Shep & The Limelights
Darlin' Be Home Soon - Joe Cocker / Lovin' Spoonful / Bobby Darin
Gypsy Woman (She's Homeless) - Crystal Waters
Homeward Bound - Simon & Garfunkel

I Can Never Go Home Anymore - Shangri Las
I Feel Like Breaking Up Somebody's Home - Ann Peebles
I Want to Walk You Home - Fats Domino
I'll Be Home - Flamingos
I'll Take You Home - Drifters
I'm Going Home - Ten Years After
I'm Going Home - Rocky Horror Picture Show
I'm Going Home - Kingston Trio
Let Me Go Home Whiskey - Amos Milburn
Long Long Way from Home - Foreigner
Making My Home Where I Hang My Hat - Johnny Copeland
My Hometown - Bruce Springsteen
She's Leaving Home - Beatles
Sorry (I Ran All the Way Home) - Impalas
Sweet Home Alabama - Lynyrd Skynyrd
Take Me Home - Cher
Take Me Home Tonight - Eddie Money
Til My Baby Comes Home - Luther Vandross
Take Me Home - Phil Collins

Hot

Fire & Ice - Pat Benetar
Heat of the Moment - Asia
Heatwave - Martha & The Vandellas
Hot Pants - James Brown
Hot for Teacher - Van Halen
Hot Child in the City - Nick Gilder
Hot Stuff - Rolling Stones
Hot Stuff - Donna Summer
Hot Hot Hot - Buster Poindexter
Hot Girls in Love - Loverboy
Hot Legs - Rod Stewart
Red Hot - Billy Lee Riley
Some Like It Hot - Power Station
Too Hot - Kool & The Gang
The Heat is On - Glenn Frey

& Cold

Baby It's Cold Outside - Ray Charles
Cool Change - Little River Band
Cold Sweat - James Brown
Cold As Ice - Foreigner
Cold Hearted - Paula Abdul
She's So Cold - Rolling Stones

Hotels

Heartbreak Hotel - Elvis
Heartbreak Hotel - Stan Freberg
Hotel Happiness - Brook Benton
Hotel California - Eagles
King of the Road - Roger Miller
Puttin' on the Ritz - Taco

Indian

Apache - Shadows / Sugar Hill Gang
Indian Giver - 1910 Fruitgum Co
Indian Reservation - Paul Revere & Raiders
Kimo-Sabe - Electric Indian (1969)
Mr. Custer - Larry Verne
Running Bear - Johnny Preston
Ten Little Indians - Beach Boys

Inspirational

Jesus is Just Alright - Doobie Brothers
Oh Happy Day - Edwin Hawkins Singers
Oh How Happy - Shades of Blue
Put Your Hand in the Hand - Ocean
Spirit in the Sky - Norman Greenbaum
Shout - Isley Brothers

Instrumentals

20-75 - Willie Mitchell

Astronauts - Baja
Apache - Shadows / Sugar Hill Gang
Boss - Rumblers
El Rancho Rock - Champs
Ghost Riders in the Sky - Ramrods
Happy Organ - Dave "Baby" Cortez
Harlem Nocturne - Viscounts
Hideaway - Freddie King
Hot Pastrami - Dartells
Let There Be Drums - Sandy Nelson
Lonely Surfer - Jack Nitzsche
Misirlou - Dick Dale & His Deltones
Perfidia - Ventures
Perculator (Twist) - Billy Joe & The Checkmates
Penetration - Pyramids
Rawhide - Link Wray & His Raymen
Red River Rock - Johnny & The Hurricanes
Rumble - Link Wray & His Raymen
Smokie (Part II) - Bill Black Combo
Slaughter On Tenth Avenue - Ventures
Shotgun - Jr. Walker & The All Stars
Sleep Walk - Santo & Johnny
Tequila - Champs
Telestar - Tornadoes
Topsy (Part II) - Cozy Cole
Tough - Ace Cannon
Walkin' with Mr. Lee - Lee Allen & His Band
Wipe Out - Surfaris
Wild Weekend - Rockin' Rebels
Wiggle Wobble - Les Cooper & The Soul Rockers
Wham - Lonnie Mack
You Can't Sit Down - Phil Upchurch Combo

Instumentals -Ventures

Walk Don't Run & Walk Don't Run '64 - Ventures
Slaughter on Tenth Ave - Ventures
Perfidia - Ventures
Hawaii Five-O - Ventures

Instrumentals - Duane Eddy

Because They're Young - Duane Eddy
Cannonball - Duane Eddy
Forty Miles of Bad Road - Duane Eddy
Peter Gunn - Duane Eddy / Dick Dale
Rebel Rouser - Duane Eddy

Instrumentals - Dick Dale

Bustin' Surfboards - Dick Dale
California Sun - Dick Dale
Ghost Riders in the Sky - Dick Dale
King of the Surf Guitar - Dick Dale
Misirlou - Dick Dale
Peter Gunn - Dick Dale
Pipeline (with Stevie Ray Vaughn)
Surf Beat - Dick Dale
Surf Rider - Dick Dale

Jailbait (Also See Sweet Sixteen)

Almost Grown - Chuck Berry
Anything by Jerry Lee Lewis
Edge of Seventeen - Stevie Nicks
Hey Little School Girl - Tom & Jerry (Simon & Garfunkel)
Good Morning Little School Girl - John Lee Hooker / Eric Clapton / Others
I'm So Young - Students
Jailbait - Andre Williams
Teenage Wildlife - David Bowie
Young Blood - Coasters
Young Girl - Gary Pluckett & The Union Gap
Young Love - Sonny James

Jailbird Blues

Chain Gang - Sam Cooke
I Fought The Law - Bobby Fuller Four
I Walk the Line - Johnny Cash
Indiana Wants Me - R. Dean Taylor

I've Got to Get a Message to You - Bee Gees
Jailhouse Rock - Elvis
Midnight Special - Johnny Rivers / CCR
Riot in Cell Block # 9 - Robins / Coasters
Tie a Yellow Ribbon - Tony Orlando & Dawn

Jungle Fever

Baby Elephant Walk - Henry Mancini / Bill Haley & His Comets
Bungle in the Jungle - Jethro Tull
Hunter Gets Captured By The Game - Marvelettes
Iko Iko - Dixie Cups
Jungle Boogie - Kool & The Gang / K.C. & The Sunshine Band
Jungleland - Bruce Springsteen
Jungle Love - Van Morrison / Steve Miller band
Jungle Love - Morris Day & The Time
Jungle Fever - Chakachas
Jungle Man - Red Hot Chili Peppers
Mama Ooh Mow Mow - Rivingtons
Papa Ooh Mow Mow - Rivingtons
Pata Pata - Miriam Makeba
Rockin' in the Jungle - Eternals
Run Through the Jungle - CCR
Stranded in the Jungle - Cadets / Jayhawks
The Lion Sleeps Tonight - Tokens / Kingston Trio / Robert John
Watusi - Vibrations / Larks
Welcome to the Jungle - Guns & Roses
Wimoweh - Weavers
Witch Docter - David Seville

Knocking

Crazy Little Mama - El Dorados
I Hear You Knocking - Lazy Lester / Smiley Lewis
I'm Going to Knock on Your Door - Eddie Hodges
Keep On Knocking - Little Richard
Knock On Wood -   Eddie Floyd / Mary Griffith
Knock Me Down - Red Hot Chilli Peppers
Knock Three Times - Tony Orlando & Dawn
Knocking On Heaven's Door - Bob Dylan

Shout Shout (Knock Yourself Out) - Ernie Maresca
Who's That Knocking - Genies

Laundromat

Leader of the Laundromat - Detergents
Laundromat Blues - Albert King
Dirty Laundry - Don Henley

Lies

Don't Play That Song (You Lied) - Ben E. King
Lies - Knickerbockers
Liar Liar - Castaways
Little Lies - Fleetwood Mac
Lies - Thompson Twins
Liar - Three Dog Night
White lies, Blue Eyes - Bullet
Would I Lie to You - Charles & Eddie

Light

2000 Light Years from Home - Rolling Stones
Blinded by the Light - Manfred Mann / Bruce Springsteen
Bright Lights, Big City - Jimmy Reed
Blue light Boogie - Louis Jordan
Dance to the Light of the Moon - Olympics
Dim the Lights - Donna Summer
Flash Light - Parliment
Harbor Lights - Platters
Heartlight - Neil Diamond
I Saw the Light - Todd Rundgren
Lights - Journey
Light My Fire - Doors / Jose Feliciano
Long as I Can See The Light - CCR
Party Lights - Claudine Clark
Shine a Light - Rolling Stones
Turn on Your Love Light - Bobby Bland
Turn Off the Lights - Teddy Pendergrass
Twilight Time - Platters

Twilight Zone - Golden Earring
When the Lovelight Starts Shining Through Your Eyes - Supremes
When the Lights Go Out - Jimmy Witherspoon
When God Shines His Light - Van Morrison

Little Artists

Alan Freed did tag "Little Anthony " with that moniker & it stuck

Little Anthony & The Imperials
Little Eva
Little Feat
Little Joey & The Thrillers
Little Johnny Taylor
Little Junior Parker
Little Milton
Little Steven & The Disciples (Grew up to be on E Street & a Soprano)
Little Stevie Wonder (He outgrew it !)
Little Willie John

Little Tunes

A Little Bit Me, A Little Bit You - Monkees
A Little Bit O'Soap - Jarmels
A Little Bit O'Soul - Music Explosion
At My Front Door (Crazy Little Mama Song) - El Dorados
Come On Little Angel - Belmonts
Come a Little Bit Closer - Jay & The Americans
Crazy Little Thing Called Love - Queen
Dance Little Sister - Terrance Trent D'Arby
Every Little Bit Hurts - Brenda Holloway
Foolish Little Girl - Shirelles
Good Morning Little School Girl - John Lee Hooker / Eric Clapton / Others
Gimme a Little Sign - Brenton Wood
Give Me Just a Little More Time - Chairman of the Board
Hey Little Cobra - Rip Chords
Hey Little Girl - Major Lance
Hey Little Girl - Dee Clark
Hello Little Girl - Beatles
I Say A Little Prayer - Aretha Franklin

I'm Gonna Love You just a Little More Baby - Barry White
I've Told Every Little Star - Linda Scott
Just a Little - Beau Brummels
I Know a Little - Lynyrd Skynyrd
Just a Little Bit - Rosco Gordon
Just a Little Too Much - Ricky Nelson
Lay a Little Lovin' on Me - Robin McNamara
Let the Little Girl Dance - Billy Bland
Little Arrows - Leapy Lee (1968)
Little Black Egg - Nightcrawlers
Little Bitty Pretty One - Thurston Harris / Dee Clark / Huey Lewis
Little Boy Sad - Johnny Burnette
Little by Little - Junior Wells
Little Darlin' - Gladiolas / Diamonds
Little Diane - Dion
Little Duece Coupe - Beach Boys
Little Egypt - Coasters
Little Girl - Syndicate of Sound
Little Girl of Mine - Cleftones
Little Honda - Hondells
Little Jeannie - Elton John
Little Old Lady from Pasadena - Jan & Dean
Little Latin Lupe Lu - Righteous Brothers
Little Lies - Fleetwood Mac
Little Red Corvette - Prince
Little Red Rooster - Howlin' Wolf
Little Sister - Elvis
Little Star - Elegants
Little Things Mean a Lot - Kitty Kallen
Little Town Flirt - Del Shannon
Little Willy - Sweet
Mother's Little Helper - Rolling Stones
My Little Red Book - Love
Poor Little Fool - Ricky Nelson
Pretty Little Girl - Monarchs
Pretty Little Angel Eyes - Curtis Lee
Put a Little Love in Your Heart - Jackie DeShannon
Rockin' Little Angel - Ray Smith
Smile a Little Smile for Me - Flying Machine
Sweet Little Rock & Roller - Chuck Berry

Sweet Little Angel - B.B. KingSweet Little Sixteen - Chuck Berry
Take Me in Your Arms (& Rock Me a Little While) - Kim Weston
The Little Girl I Once Knew - Beach Boys
This Little Voice - A.C. Reed & Earl Hooker
This Little Girl - Gary US Bonds
Too Much, Too Little, Too Late - Johnny Mathis & Deneice Williams
Try a Little Tenderness - Otis Redding
Wake Up Little Susie - Everly Brothers
When My Little Girl is Smiling - Drifters
With a Little Help from My Friends - Beatles / Joe Cocker

Lonely

Have You Ever Been Lonely - Patsy Cline
Hey There Lonely Girl - Eddie Holman
I've Been Lonely Too Long - Rascals
Just Ask the Lonely - Four Tops
Just Don't Want to Be Lonely - Main Ingredient
Lonely Avenue - Ray Charles
Lonely Boy - Paul Anka
Lonely Surfer - Jack Nitzche
Lonely Teardrops - Jackie Wilson
Lonely Weekends - Charlie Rich
Love or Let Me Be Lonely - Friends of Distinction
Mr. Lonely - Bobby Vinton
New York's a Lonely Town - Tradewinds
Only the Lonely - Motels
Only the Lonely - Roy Orbison
Owner of a Lonely Heart - Yes
Sgt Pepper's Lonely Hearts Club Band - Beatles
Those Lonely Lonely Nights - Earl King

Lonesome

Are You Lonesome Tonight - Elvis Presley
I'm So Lonesome I Could Cry - B.J. Thomas
Lonesome Town - Ricky Nelson
Lonesome Loser - Little River Band
Oh Lonesome Me - Don Gibson

Louie Louie (& Artists Who Recorded It)

Greatest Garage Band Rock Song Ever Made - Done by more artists than just about anybody. It was written by Richard Berry, a singer song writer who was a member of the Robins, a West coast harmony group that were the predecessors to the Coasters. He sand the lead on their big hit "Riot in Cell Block # 9 ". He recorded It in 1957 as Richard Berry & the Pharoahs. It became a regional favorite in the Northwest, by Rockin' Robin Roberts & The Wailers. He was the one responsible for the guitar solo at the break. It was also recorded by two Oregon groups Paul Revere & The Raiders from Seattle, who later had great success & a string of classic hits & were the house band for a time with Dick Clark's American Bandstand & "Where the Action Is" & The Kingsmen from Portland. They recorded the song within months of one another. The Kingsmen had the biggest National success taking the song to # 2 in 1963. It was kept out of the #1 spot by The Singing Nun - Dominique , ...can you say, "Divine Intervention" ? The United States Senate even conducted an in depth investigation, because the lyrics were thought to be dirty. Talk about great publicity !!!. Our tax dollars at work! It was really just a Caribbean Love Song about a sailor home from the sea, missing his girl with the rose in her hair written by Richard Berry. There are more than a thousand renditions of this " garage rock " anthem. Here are a few of the notable contributions listed by artist & I imagine there are many many many more:

Algarette
Archies
Australian Crawl
Bad Religion
Barry White
Beach Boys
Beatles
Beausoleil (Cajun)
Black Flag
Blondie
Blue Comets
Bob Marley & The Wailers
Bruce Springsteen
Budweiser Frogs
Clash
Covers

Cramps
Cult
Dave Matthews Band
Don & The Goodtimes
Doors
Eddie & The Subtitles
Eläkeläiset
Falcons
Fantastic Plastic Machine
Fat Boys
Flamin' Groovies
Floyd Cramer
Frank Zappa / UncleMeat
Grateful Dead
Henry Lee Summer
Husker Du
Iggy Pop
Ike & Tina Turner
Impossibles (The Hallelouie Chorus)
Jan & Dean
Jim Capaldi
Joan Jett
John Belushi (Animal House)
Johnny Winter
Julie London
Kingsmen (The Most Famous Version & Their Biggest Hit)
Kinks
Kiss (MTV Unplugged)
Led Zeppelin
Les Dantz & His Orchestra
Little Bill & The Blue Notes
Mark Bradford (Pharoah Pharoah)
Me First & The Gimme Gimmes
Mongo Santamaria Band
Motorhead
Murf the Surf & The Surfettes
Night Train Revue
O.A.R.
Operation Ivy
Otis Redding

Patti Smith
Paul Keinitz (Shock the Louie)
Paul Revere & The Raiders
Pete Fountain
Pow Wow - regagner les plaines (accapella)
Queers
R.E.M.
Red Square (Russian Version)
Rice University Marching Owl Band
Richard Berry & The Pharoahs (Composer 1956)
Robert Plant
Rockin' Robin Roberts & The Wailers (Original Famous Guitar Solo)
Sandpipers
Shockwaves (Surfin' Louie)
Sonics
Standells
Stanely Clarke & George Duke
Stewart & Gaskin
Stooges
Swamp Rats
Tams
Time Code with Steve Sparling
Teenage Head
The Last
39 Clocks
The Three Amigos
Thunderclap Newman
Tom Petty
Toots & The Maytals
Travis Wammack
Troggs (Wild Thing was a "Louie Louie" Clone)
Tuck Andress
University of Washington Husky Marching Band
University of Wisconsin Marching Band
Ventures
Weezer
West Coast Pop Art Experimental Band

Love (Biggest Category, What Better Reason to Write A Song)

'65 Love Affair - Paul Davis
A Teenager in Love - Dion & The Belmonts
A Fool in Love - Ike & Tina Turner
A Big Hunk O'Love - Elvis
A World Without Love - Peter & Gordon
A Groovy Kind of Love - Wayne Fontana & The Mindbenders
A Thing Called Love - Bonnie Raitt
A Love Song - Anne Murray
A Woman Needs Love (Just Like You Do) - Ray Parker Jr.
ABC's of Love - Frankie Lymon & The Teenagers
Addicted to Love - Robert Palmer
After the Love Has Gone - Earth, Wind & Fire
After the Loving - Englebert Humperdinck
All Out of Love - Air Supply
All I Want to Do is Make Love to You - Heart
All My Loving - Beatles
All You Need is Love - Beatles
And I Love Her - Beatles
And I Love You So - Don McLean
April Love - Pat Boone
Are You Going To Be There (At the Love-In) - Chocolate Watch Band

Baby Love - Supremes
Baby I Love You - Aretha Franklin
Baby I Love Your Way - Peter Fampton
Baby I Love Your Way / Freebird (Free Baby) - Will To Power
Best of My Love - Emotions
Big Love - Fleetwood Mac
Book of Love - Monotones
Bye Bye Love - Everly Brothers

Can't Help Falling in Love - Elvis
Can't Get Enough of Your Love Baby - Barry White
Can't Buy Me Love - Beatles
Caribbean Queen (No More Love on the Run) - Billy Ocean
Chapel of Love - Dixie Cups
Chuck E's In Love - Rickie Lee Jones
Could It Be I'm Falling in Love - Spinners

Could Never Love Another After Loving You - Temptations
Come & Get Your Love - Redbone
Cradle of Love - Johnny Preston
Crazy Love - Poco
Crazy Little Thing Called Love - Queen

Dedicated to the One I Love - Five Royales / Shirelles / Mamas & Papas
Do You Believe in Love - Huey Lewis & The News
Do You Love Me - Contours
Don't Throw Your Love on Me So Strong - Albert Green
Don't Let Them Take Your Love From Me - Four Tops
Don't Throw Your Love Away - Searchers
Down the Aisle of Love - Quintones
Double Shot (Of My Baby's Love) - Swinging Medallions

Eddie My Love - Teen Queens
Endless Love - Diana Ross & Lionel Richie
Everybody Loves a Clown - Gary Lewis & The Playboys
Everybody's Got a Right to Love - Supremes
Everlasting Love - Robert John / Carl Carlton
Everybody Needs Somebody to Love - Solomon Burke
Everybody Loves to Cha Cha Cha - Sam Cooke
Everybody Loves a Lover - Shirelles
(Every Time I Turn Around) I'm in Love Again - LTD

Fallin' in Love - Souther Hillman Furey Band
Falling in Love with Love - Supremes
Feel Like Makin' Love - Bad Company
Fooled Around & Fell in Love - Elvin Bishop
For Your Love - Ed Townsend
For Your Precious Love - Jerry Butler & The Impressions
For The Love of Money - O'Jays
For Your Love - Yardbirds
Freeway of Love - Aretha Franklin

Game of Love - Wayne Fontana & The Mindbenders
Gangster of Love - Johnny " Guitar " Watson
Gangster of Love - Steve Miller
(Girls, Girls, Girls) Were Made to Love - Eddie Hodges
Goodnight My Love - Jesse Belvin

Good Lovin' Gone Bad - Bad Company
Glory of Love - Peter Cetera

Hallelujah I Love Her So - Ray Charles / Beatles
Have You Ever Loved a Woman - Freddy King
Hello I Love You - Doors
Hey Love - Delphonics
Higher Love - Steve Winwood
Heard It in a Love Song - Marshall Tucker Band
Honey Love - Drifters with Clyde McPhatter
Hot Girls in Love - Loverboy
How Deep is Your Love - Bee Gees
How Sweet It Is to Be Loved By You - Marvin Gaye / James Taylor
How Sweet It Is (To Be Loved By You) - Marvin Gaye
How's Your Love Life Baby - Ted Taylor
Hula Love - Buddy Knox

(I Wanna) Love My Life Away - Gene Pitney
I Can't Quit Your Love - Four Tops
I Can't Make You Love Me - Bonnie Raitt
I Can't Stop Loving You - Ray Charles
I Do Love You - Billy Stewart
I Don't Want to Live Without Your Love -Chicago
I Just Want to Make Love to You - Muddy Waters
I Feel Love - Donna Summer
I Know (You Don't Love Me No More) - Barbara George
I Love the Nightlife (Disco Round) - Alicia Bridges
I Love You So - Chantels
I Love You - Volumes
I Love You - People
I Love Music (Part I) - O'Jays
I Love How You Love Me - Paris Sisters
I Love You So Much It Hurts - Patsy Cline
I Love You 1000 Times - Platters
I Love You Because - Platters
I Love You Honey - John Lee Hooker
I Love the Way You Love - Marv Johnson
I Need Your Love Tonight - Elvis
I Never Loved a Man (The Way I Loved You) - Aretha Franklin /Commitme
I Really Love You - Stereos

I Think I Love You - Partridge Family
I Want Your Love - Chic
I Want You, I Need You, I Love You - Elvis
I Want to Know What Love Is - Foreigner
I Wanna Love Him So Bad - Jelly Beans
I Was Made to Love Her - Stevie Wonder
I Will Always Love You - Whitney Houston
I'd Really Love to See You Tonight - England Dan & John Ford Coley
I'd Love to Change The World - Ten Years After
I'm Gonna Make You Love Me - Supremes & Temptations
I'm Still in Love with You - Al Green
I'm in Love - Aretha Franklin
I'm Not in Love - 10cc
I'm in Love Again - Fats Domino
I'll Always Love You - Taylor Dane
I'll Have to Say I Love You in a Song - Jim Croce
I'm Still in Love with You - Al Green
I'm in Love - Aretha Franklin
I'm Not in Love - 10cc
I'm in Love Again - Fats Domino
I've Got Love if You Want It - Slim Harpo
If You Really Love Me - Stevie Wonder
If I Had A Love - Platters
If You Love Me Like You Say - Little Jonny Taylor
In & Out of Love - Supremes
Is This Love - Survivor
Is This Love - Whitesnake
It Hurts to Be in Love - Gene Pitney
It's Only Love - Beatles
It's Only Love - Bryan Adams

Jump (For My Love) - Pointer Sisters
Jungle Love - Van Morrison

(Love is Like a) Heatwave - Martha Reeves & The Vandellas
L-O-V-E - Al Green
La La Means I Love You - Delfonics
Lay All Your Love on Me - ABBA
Lady Love - Robin Trower
Let Love Come Between Us - James & Bobby Purify

Let Me Love You Tonight - Pure Prairie League
Like to Live the Love - B.B. King
Look of Love - ABC
Looking for Love - Johnny Lee / Bobby Womack
Looking Through The Eyes of Love - Gene Pitney
Lost in Love - Air Supply
Lotta Love - Nicollette Larson
Love is Alive - Gary Wright
Love Potion # 9 - Clovers / Searchers
Love Boat - Jack Jones
Love Calling - Billy Idol
Love Came to Me - Dion
Love Child - Supremes
Love's Theme - Love Unlimited Orchestra
Love Ballad - LTD
Love Grows (Where My Rosemary Goes) - Edison Lighthouse
Love Hangover - Diana Ross
Love Her Madly - Doors
Love is All Around - Troggs
Love is a Drug - Roxy Music
Love is a Rose - Linda Ronstadt
Love is in the Air - John Paul Young
Love is Here & Now You're Gone - Supremes
Love is Like An Itching in My Heart - Supremes
Love is Like Oxygen - Sweet
Love is a Hurtin' Thing - Lou Rawls
Love is Strange - Mickey & Sylvia
Love is Sweeter Than Wine - Four Tops
Love is Sweeter Than Ever - Four Tops
LoveLove is Like a Rock - Donny Iris
Love in an Elevator - Aerosmith
Love Letters - Ketty Lester
Love Makes the World Go Round - Deon Jackson
Love Me Tender - Elvis
Love Me - Elvis
Love Me Tomorrow - Chicago
Loves Me Like a Rock - Paul Simon
Love Me Two Times - Doors
Love Machine - Smokey Robinson & The Miracles
Love Makes a Woman - Barbara Acklin

Love Me Do - BeatlesLove In Vain - Rolling Stones
Love My Baby - Little Junior's Blue Flames
Love Reign O'er Me - Who
Love Rollercoaster - Ohio Players
Love Letters in the Sand - Pat Boone
Love Stinks - J. Geils Band
Love Shack - B-52s
Love Sneakin' Up On You - Bonnie Raitt
Love Train - O'Jays
Love the One Your With - Stephen Stills
Love to Love You Baby - Donna Summer
Love Will Keep Us Together - Captain & Tennile
Love Will Find A Way - Pablo Cruise
Love Will Tear Us Apart - Joy Division
Love Won't Let Me Wait - Major Harris
Love Woke Me Up This Morning - Temptations
Love Will Lead You Back - Taylor Dane
Love You So - Ron Holden
Love & Happiness - Toots & The Maytals
Lovin' Touchin' Sqeezin' - Journey
Lovin' You - Minnie Riperton

Making Love Out of Nothing at All - Air Supply
Mio Amore (My Love Till The End of Time) - Flamingos
Mighty Love - Spinners
Modern Love - David Bowie
My Baby Loves Lovin' - White Plains
Mountain of Love - Harold Dorman / Johnny Rivers
My Own True Love - Duprees
My Pledge of Love - Joe Jeffrey Group
My True Love - Jack Scott
My Love Will Never Die - Otis Rush
Muskrat Love - Captain & Tennile

Need Your Love So Bad - Little Willie John
Never Ending Song of Love - Delaney & Bonnie & Friends
Never My Love - Association

Only Love Can Break a Heart - Gene Pitney
Ooh Wee Baby I love You - Fred Hughes

One Love - Bob Marley & The Wailers
One of a Kind (Love Affair) - Spinners

Part Time Lover - Little Johnny Taylor
Please Return Your Love To Me - Temptations
Please Send Me Someone to Love - Moonglows / Percy Mayfield
Please Accept My Love - B.B. King
Please Love Me Forever - Cathy Jean & The Roomates
Pledging My Love - Johnny Ace
Power of Love - Huey Lewis & The News
Put a Little Love in Your Heart - Jackie DeShannon
Puppy love - Paul Anka

Radar Love - Golden Earring
Real Love - Beatles
Ready for Love - Bad Company
Real Love - Doobie Brothers
Rockin' Good Way (To Mess Around & Fall in Love) - Dinah
Washington & Brook Benton

Say You Love Me - Fleetwood Mac
Sea of Love - Phil Phillips / Honeydrippers
Searching for My Love - Bobby Moore & The Rythmn Aces
Share Your Love with Me - Aretha Franklin
Share Your Love with Me - Aretha Franklin
Shower Me with Your Love - Surface
She Loves You - Beatles
Sit Down I Think I Love You - Mojo Men
Soldier of Love - Donny Osmond
Somebody to Love - Jefferson Airplane
Standing in the Shadows of Love - Four Tops
Standing at the Crossroads of Love - Supremes
Stoned Love - Supremes
Stop in the Name of Love - Supremes
So Sad (To Watch Good Love Go Bad) - Everly Brothers
Softly Whispering I Love You - English Congregation
Somebody to Love - Queen
Sunshine of Your Love - Cream

Tainted Love - Soft Cell

Ten Commandments of Love - Moonglows
That's the Way Love Is - Bobby Bland
That's Why (I Love You So) - Jackie Wilson
The Glory of Love - Five Keys
The Love I Lost - Harold Melvin & The Blue Notes
The Love of My Man - Theola Gilgore
The Things We Do for Love - 10cc
The Love You Save (May Be Your Own) - Joe Tex
The One Who Really Loves You - Mary Wells
The One That You Love - Air Supply
Thin Line Between Love & Hate - Persuaders
To Sir with Love - Lulu
To Know Him is to Love Him - Teddy Bears
That's The Way Love Is - Marvin Gaye
This Will Be (An Everlasting Love) - Natalie Cole
There Goes Another Love Song - Outlaws
To Be a Lover - Billy Idol
Tonight's All Right for Love - Elvis
Tonight I fell in Love - Tokens
Treasure of Love - Clyde McPhatter
True Love Ways - Buddy Holly
True Love Never Runs Smooth - Gene Pitney
(If You Cry) True Love True Love - Drifters
True Love - Patsy Cline
The Love You Save - Jackson Five
Two Divided By Love - Grass Roots
Tunnel of Love - Dire Straits
Turn On Your Love Light - Bobby Bland

Walk Away from Love - David Ruffin
Warm & Tender Love - Percy Sledge
Wedding Song (There is Love) - Peter, Paul & Mary / Lettermen /
Captain & Tennille
Without Love (There is Nothing) - Clyde McPhatter
Will You Love Me Tomorrow - Shirelles
Will You Still Love Me - Chicago
Without the One You Love (Life is Not Worth Living) - Four Tops
What's Love Got to Do with It - Tina Turner
What's So Funny 'Bout Peace, Love & Understanding - Elvis Costello
What The World Needs Now is Love - Jackie DeShannon

What Does It Take (To Win Your Love) - Jr. Walker & All Stars
When Love Calls - Atlantic Starr
When Will I Be Loved - Linda Ronstadt
When a Man Loves a Woman - Percy Sledge
When the Lovelight Starts Shining Through His Eyes - Supremes
When Your In Love with a Beautiful Woman - Dr. Hook
Where Did Our Love Go - Supremes
Who Loves You - Four Seasons
Who Do You Love - Bo Diddley
Who's Makin' Love - Johnny Taylor
Why Does Love Got to Be So Sad - Derek & The Dominoes
Why Do Fools Fall in Love - Frankie Lymon & Teenagers
Why Can't This Be Love - Van Halen
Words of Love - Buddy Holly / Mamas & the Papas
Whole Lotta Love - Led Zeppelin

You'll Never Find Another Love Like Mine - Lou Rawls
You Need Love Like I Do Don't You - Gladys Knight & The Pips
(Your Love Keeps Lifting Me) Higher & Higher - Jackie Wilson
Young & In Love - Dick & Dee Dee
You Always Hurt The One You Love - Clarence " Frogman " Henry
You've Got to Hide Your Love Away - Beatles
You Gotta Have Love in Your Heart - Four Tops & Supremes
Your Precious Love - Marvin Gaye & Tammi Terrell
Young Love - Sonny James
You Can't Hurry Love - Supremes
Your Wonderful Sweet Sweet Love - Supremes
You Don't Love Me - Willie Cobbs
Your Love - Outfield
Young Love - Tab Hunter

& the Ultimate: Silly Love Songs - Paul McCartney & Wings

Lovers

A Lover's Question - Clyde McPhatter
Distant Lover - Marvin Gaye
Dream Lover - Bobby Darin
Fifty Ways to Leave Your Lover - Paul Simon
Friends & Lovers - Gloria Loring & Carl Anderson

Imaginary Lover - Atlanta Rythmn Section
Lover's Island - Blue Jays
Loverboy - Billy Ocean
Lover's Holiday - Peggy Scott & Jo Jo Benson
Lovergirl - Teena Marie
Lover's Concerto - Toys
Lovers Never Say Goodbye - Flamingos
Lover Please - Clyde McPhatter
Lovers Who Wander - Dion
No Tell Lover - Chicago
Penny Lover - Lionel Ritchie
Secret Lovers - Atlantic Starr
Torn Between Two Lovers - Mary MacGregor
Two Lovers - Mary Wells
Young Lovers - Paul & Paula

Love (By Oneself)

Captain Jack - Billy Joel
I Think I'm Turning Japanese - Vapors
Pictures of Lili - Who
Pump It Up - Elvis Costello
She Bop - Cyndy Lauper
Shock the Monkey - Peter Gabriel
Shake a Hand - Faye Adams

Magic

Black Magic Woman - Fleetwood Mac / Santana
Could This Be Magic - Dubs
Do You Believe in Magic - Lovin' Spoonful
Magic - Pilot
Magic - Cars
Magic - Olivia Newton John
Magic Bus - Who
Magic Carpet Ride - Steppenwolf
Magical Mystery Tour - Beatles
My Baby Must Be a Magician - Marvelettes
Spanish Castle Magic - Jimi Hendrix Experience
Strange Magic - ELO

The Magic Touch - Platters
This Magic Moment - Drifters / Jay & The Americans
You Made Me Believe in Magic - Bay City Rollers

Mail Tunes

Dear One - Larry Finegan
I'm Gonna Sit Right Down & Write Myself a Letter - Billy Williams
Please Mr. Postman - Marvelettes / Beatles / Carpenters
Letter Full of Tears - Gladys Knight & Pips
Letter from My Darling - Little Willie John
Letter to an Angel - Jimmy Clanton
Letter to Myself - Chilites
Love Letters - Ketty Lester
Love Letter in the Sand - Pat Boone
Mailman Bring Me No More Blues - Buddy Holly
Mailman Blues - Lloyd Price
PS I Love You - Beatles
Postman Blues - Dinah Washington
Return to Sender - Elvis
Sealed with a Kiss - Brian Hyland
Send Me Some Lovin' - Sam Cooke
Signed, Sealed, Delivered I'm Yours - Stevie Wonder
Seven Letters - Ben E. King
Special Delivery - 1910 Fruitgum Company
The Letter - Boxtops / Joe Cocker
Tears on Your Letter - Hank Ballard & Midnighters
Teenage Letter - Jerry Lee Lewis / Joe Turner
The Glory of Love - Velvetones
Take a Letter Maria - R.B. Greaves
Twistin' Postman - Marvelettes
Western Union - Five Americans
Western Union Man - Jerry Butler
Zip Code - Five Americans

Mama's Advice

Mama Told Me Not To Come - Three Dog Night
Mama Didn't Lie - Jan Bradley
Mama Said - Shirelles

Mama Talk to Your Daughter - J.B. Lenoir
Shop Around - Miracles
Your Mother Should Know - Beatles

Mama

At My Front Door (Crazy Little Mama Song) - El Dorados
Crazy Mama - J.J. Cale
Have You Seen Your Mother Baby (Standing in the Shadows) -
Rolling Stones
Fujiyama Mama - Wanda Jackson
Hey Lawdy Mama - Steppenwolf
I'll Always Love My Mama - Intruders
Mama - Connie Francis
Mama (He Treats Your Daughter Mean) - Ruth Brown
Mama Ooh Mow Mow - Rivingtons
Mamamia - ABBA
Mother in Law - Ernie K. Doe
Mother & Child Reunion - Paul Simon
Motherless Child - Eric Clapton
Mother's Little Helper - Rolling Stones
Mrs. Brown You've Got a Lovely Daughter - Herman's Hermits
She's a Bad Mama Jama - Carl Carlton
Sylvia's Mother - Dr. Hook & The Medicine Show
Tell Mama - Etta James
Your Mama Don't Dance (& Your Daddy Don't Rock & Roll) -
Loggins & Messina

& Papa

My Dad - Paul Peterson
Oh My Papa - Eddie Fisher
Papa Don't Take No Mess - James Brown
Papa's Got a Brand New Bag - James Brown
Papa Don't Preach - Madonna
Papa Ooh Mow Mow - Rivingtons
Papa Was a Rolling Stone - Temptations

Man

A Man Needs His Lovin' - Anson Funderburgh
Back Door Man - Howling Wolf / Doors
Big Boss Man - Jimmy Reed
Big Man in Town - Four Seasons
Big Man in Town - Four Seasons
Blind Man - Little Milton
Blue Collar Man (Long Nights) - Styx
Brown Eyed Handsome Man - Chuck Berry
Crazy Man Crazy - Bill Haley & His Comets
Dead man's Curve - Jan & Dean
Dirty Man - Laura Lee
Do Right Woman, Do Right Man - Aretha Franklin
Family Man - Hall & Oates
Forever Man - Eric Clapton
Fat Man - Jethro Tull
Guitar Man - Bread
Glory for Man - Robert J. Lockwood
Gypsy Man - War
Hard Drivin' Man - J. Geils Band
Handy Man - Jimmy Jones / James Taylor
Hey Western Union Man - Jerry Butler
Hot Rod Man - Ted Rabinowitz
Hoochie Coochie Man - Muddy Waters / Eric Clapton
Hound Dog Man - Fabian
Hurdy Gurdy Man - Donovan
I Need a Man - Grace Jones
I Guess I'll Miss the Man - Supremes
I'm a Man - Bo Diddley
I'm Your Boogie Man - KC & The Sunshine Band
I'm the Man - Joe Jackson
Ice Cream Man - Van Halen
It's a Man's, Man's, Man's World James Brown
I'm a Man - Spencer Davis Group / Yardbirds
Lucky Man - Emerson, Lake & Palmer
Macho Man - Village People
Madman Across the Water - Elton John
Man in the Mirror - Michael Jackson
Manish Boy - Muddy Waters

Middle Man - Living Colour
Mr. Tambourine Man - Byrds
Mr. Bass Man - Johnny Cymbal
Neanderthal Man - Hot Legs
Never Loved a Man (The Way I Loved You) - Aretha Franklin
New World Man - Rush
Nowhere Man - Beatles
Ol' Man River - Temptations
Piano Man - Billy Joel
Please Mr. Postman - Marvelettes
Poetry Man - Phoebe Snow
Pouring Water on a Drowning Man - James Carr
Ramblin' Man - Allman Brothers
Real Man - Todd Rundgren
Rubberband Man - Spinners
Secret Agent Man - Johnny Rivers
Sharp Dressed Man - ZZ Top
Soul Man - Sam & Dave
Rocket Man - Elton John
Stand By Your Man - Tammy Wynette
Street Fighting Man - Rolling Stones
Son of a Preacher Man - Dusty Springfield
Say Man - Bo Diddley
Sixty Minute Man - Dominoes
St. Elmo's Fire (Man in Motion) - John Parr
Taxman - Beatles
The Fat Man - Fats Domino
The Man Who Shot Liberty Valence - Gene Pitney
The Charming Man - Smiths
The Love of My Man - Theola Gilgore
Tin Man - America Transformer Man - Neil Young
Trouble Man - Marvin Gaye
Travelin' Man - Ricky Nelson
Troglodyte (Cave man) - Jimmy Castor Band
Union Man - Cates Brothers
Walk Like a Man - Four Seasons
Walk Like A Man - Four Seasons / Grand Funk Railroad
Wanna Be Your Man - Beatles
Well Respected Man - Kinks
What Kind of Man Would I Be - Chicago

When A Man Loves a Woman - Percy Sledge / Michael Bolton
When I Grow Up to Be A Man - Beach Boys

Mercy Me

Have Mercy Baby - Billy Ward & The Dominoes
Mercy, Mercy - Don Covay & The Goodtimers
Mercy, Mercy, Mercy - Larry Williams & Johnny Watson
Mercy, Mercy, Mercy - Cannonball Adderley
Mercey, Mercy, Mercy - Buckinghams
Mercy, Mercy (The Ecology) - Marvin Gaye

Midnight Songs

After Midnight - Eric Clapton
In the Midnight Hour - Wilson Pickett / Commitments
I'm a Midnight Mover - Wilson Pickett
Midnight Special - Johnny Rivers / CCR
Midnight Train to Georgia - Gladys Knight & Pips
Midnight Confessions - Grass Roots
Midnight Rider - Greg Allman / Joe Cocker
Midnight Blue - Lou Gramm
Midnight at The Oasis - Maria Muldaur
Midnight Mary - Joe Powers
Midnight Blue - Melissa Manchester
Midnight Rambler - Rolling Stones
Midnight Stroll - Revels
Three Hours Past Midnight - Johhny "Guitar" Watson
Walkin' After Midnight - Patsy Cline

Mine (Can You Dig It ? .... OK, Bad Pun)

Big Bad John - Jimmy Dean
Canary in a Coal Mine - Police
NY Mining Disaster 1941 - Bee Gees
Sixteen Tons - Tennesee Ernie Ford
Working in a Coal Mine - Lee Dorsey

Money

Don't Bet Money Honey - Linda Scott
First I Look at the Purse - Contours
For the Love of Money - Ojays
Lawyers, Guns & Money - Warren Zevon
Money Honey - Clyde McPhatter & Drifters / Elvis
Money for Nothing - Dire Straits
Money (That's What I Want) - Barrett Strong / Beatles / Kingsmen /
John Belushi (Animal House Snd Trk)
Take the Money & Run - Steve Miller

Moon

Bad Moon Rising - CCR
Black Moon - Emerson, Lake & Palmer
Blue Moon - Marcels
Dance to the Light of the Moon - Olympics
Dancing in the Moonlight - King Harvest
Dark Moon - Bonnie Guitar
Everyone's Gone to the Moon - Jonathon King (1965)
Fly Me to the Moon - Bobby Darin
Moondance - Van Morrison
There's a Moon Out Tonight - Capris

& Moonlight

Moonlight Bay - Beatles
Moonlight Cocktails - Rivieras
Moonlight Feels Right - Starbuck
Mr. Moonlight - Beatles / Dr. Feelgood & The Interns

Motorcycle (Chrome Pony)

Bad Motorcycle - Storie Sisters
Born to Be Wild - Steppenwolf
Black Denim Trousers & Motorcycle Boots - Cheers
Leader of the Pack - Shangri Las
Little Honda - Hondells
Low Rider - War

Motorcycle Song - Arlo Guthrie
Motorcycle Mama - Sailcat

Mountains

Ain't No Mountain High Enough - Marvin Gaye & Tammi Terrell /
Diana Ross
Climb Every Mountain - Four Tops
Girl from Wolverton Mountain - Jo Ann Campbell
Over the Mountain, Across the Sea - Johnny & Joe
Mountain of Love - Harold Dorman / Johnny Rivers
Rocky Mountain Way - Joe Walsh
Rocky Mountain High - John Denver
River Deep, Mountain High - Supremes & Four Tops
Rocky Mountain Way - Joe Walsh
Up on the Mountain - Magnificents
Wolverton Mountain - Claude King

& Hills

A Fool on the Hill - Beatles
Blueberry Hill - Fats Domino
King of the Hill - Roy Pinette & Oak
Over the Hills & Far Away - Led Zeppelin
One Tree Hill - U2
Solsbury Hill - Peter Gabriel

Mr.

Being For the Benefit of Mr. Kite - Beatles
Dancing with Mr. D - Rolling Stones
Dear Mr. Fantasy - Traffic
I Shot Mr. Lee - Bobettes
Mr. Bass Man - Johnny Cymbal
Mr. Big Stuff - Jean Knight
Mr. Bojangles - Nitty Gritty Dirt Band
Mr. Blue - Fleetwoods
Mr. Custer - Larry Verne
Mr. Dieingly Sad - Critters
Mr. Lee - The Bobettes

Mr. Lonely - Bobby Vinton
Mr. Moonlight - Dr. Feelgood & The Interns / Beatles
Mr. Pitiful - Otis Redding
Mr. Roboto - Styx
Mr. Soul - Neil Young
Mr. Tambourine Man - Byrds
No More Mr. Nice Guy - Alice Cooper
Please Mr. Postman - Marvelettes
Walkin' with Mr. Lee - Lee Allen & His Band

& Mrs

Me & Mrs. Jones - Billy Paul
Mrs. Brown You've Got a Lovely Daughter - Herman's Hermits
Mrs. Robinson - Simon & Garfunkel

Night

A Hard Days Night - Beatles
All Day & All of the Night - Kinks
All Night Long - Lionel Ritchie
December 1963 (Oh What a Night) - Four Seasons
Even the Nights Are Better - Air Supply
Good Night - Beatles
Heat of the Night - Bryan Adams
Hollywood Nights - Bob Seger
I Love the Nightlife (Disco Round) - Alicia Bridges
In the Air Tonight - Phil Collins
In the Still of the Nite - Five Satins
Into The Night - Benny Mardones
Into the Night - B.B. King
Livin' It Up (Friday Night) - Bell & James
Night Life - B.B. King
Night Fever - Bee Gees
Night Moves - Bob Seger
Night Time is the Right Time - Ray Charles
Night Train - Jimmy Forrest
Nights in White Satin - Moody Blues
One Night - Elvis
Oh What a Night - Dells

Rainy Night in Georgia - Brook Benton
Right Time of the Night - Jennifer Warnes
Rock & Roll All Night - KissSaturday Night - Bay City Rollers
Such a Night - Bunny Paul / Drifters / Elvis
The Night is Still Young - Billy Joel
The Night Has a 1000 Eyes - Bobby Vee
You Shook Me All Night Long - AC/DC

NO

Ain't No Mountain High Enough - Diana Ross / Marvin Gaye & Tammi Terrel
Ain't No Stoppin' Us Now - McFadden & Whitehead
Ain't No Sunshine - Bill Withers
Ain't No Woman Like the One I Got - Four Tops
Caribbean Queen (No More Love on the Run) - Billy Ocean
Don't Come Around Here No More - Tom Petty & The Heartbreakers
I Can't Get No Satisfaction - Rolling Stones
I Can't Go For That (No Can Do) - Hall & Oates
I Can't Stand It No More - Peter Frampton
Miles From Nowhere - Cat Stevens
No One is to Blame - Howard Jones
No Matter What Sign You Are - Supremes
No Reply - Beatles
No Sugar Tonight / New Mother Nature - Guess Who
No Sympathy - Peter Tosh
No Time This Time - Police
No Time - Guess Who
No Tell Lover - Chicago
No Particular Place to Go - Chuck Berry
No Man's Land - Billy Joel
No Women, No Cry - Bob Marley
No Business - Bonnie RaittNowhere Man - Beatles
Papa Don't Take No Mess - James Brown
See No Evil - Television
Tell Her No - Zombies
You're No Good - Betty Everett / Linda Ronstadt

& Yes

Yes - Merry Clayton (Dirty Dancing Snd Trk)
Yes Baby - Big Mama Thornton & Johnny Ace
Yes, I'm Ready - Barbara Mason / Teri Desario
Yes It Is - Beatles
Yes, We Can Can - Pointer Sisters

Nobody

Ain't Nobody Home - Howard Tate
I Ain't Got Nobody to Love - Masqueraders
I Ain't Got Nobody - David Lee Roth
Don't Let Nobody Turn You Around - Steve Miller Band
Nobody But Me - Isley Brothers / Human Beinz
Nobody But You - Dee Clark

Nothing

Ain't Nothin' You Can Do - Bobby Bland
Ain't Nothing Like the Real Thing - Marvin Gaye & Tammi Terrell
Ain't Seen Nothing Yet - BTO
Don't Say Nothin' Bad About My Baby - Cookies
I (Who Have Nothing) - Ben E. King / Terry Knight & The Pack
Ain't Got Nothin' - Temptations
Money For Nothing - Dire Straits
Nothing From Nothing - Billy Preston
Nothin' Shakin' - Eddy Fontaine
Nothing But a Heartache - Flirtations
Nothing But a Good Time Poisin
Nothings Gonna Stop Us Now - Starship
Nothing to Do But Today - Steven Stills
Nothings Too Good for My Baby - Stevie Wonder
Nothing But Heartaches- Supremes
Nothing Takes the Place of You - Toussaint McCall
Sweet Nothin's - Brenda Lee
TAin't Nothin' To Me - Coasters
We Ain't Got Nothing Yet - Blues Magoos
Without Love There is Nothing - Clyde McPhatter

Nonsense Syllables (I Love This Category too)

Abba Zaba - Captain Beefheart
Boogie Oogie Oogie - Taste of Honey
Click Clack - Dickey Doo & The Don'ts
Da Doo Ron Ron - Crystals
Do, Re, Mi - Lee Dorsey
Do Wah Ditty - Manfred Mann
Do Wacka Do - Roger Miller
Dum Dum Song - Redcoats
Fa Fa Fa Fa Fa Fa - Otis Redding
Hi Di Ho - Blood, Sweat & Tears
Iko Iko - Dixie Cups
In-a-Gadda-Da-Vida - Iron Butterfly
Ka Ding Dong - G Clefs
La La La La La - Blendells
La Dee Dah - Billie & Lillie
Mama-Ooh-Mow Mow - Rivingtons
Mah Na Mah Na - Piero Umiliani (1977)
Nobody But Me - Human Beinz
Na Na Hey Hey - Steam
Nee Nee Na Na Nu Nu - Dickey Doo & The Don'ts
Obla Di Obla Da - Beatles
Oogum Boogum Song - Brenton Wood
Ooh Poo Pah Doo (Parts I & II) - Jesse Hill
Ooo Wee Baby - Ivy Tones
Papa-Ooh-Mow Mow - Rivingtons
Rama Lama Ding Dong - Edsels
Shama Lama Ding Dong - Otis Day & His Knights
Shoo-Bee-Doo-Bee-Doo-Dah-Day - Stevie Wonder
Sh-Boom - Chords / Crewcuts / Stan Freberg
Shoop Shoop Song (It's in His Kiss) - Betty Everett / Cher
Sha La La (Make Me Happy) - Al Green
Shimmy Shimmy Ko Ko Bop - Little Anthony & The Imperials
Ta Ta - Clyde McPhatter
Tutti Fruiti - Little Richard
Tra La La La Suzy - Jan & Dean
Ti Nee Ni Nee Nu - Slim Harpo
Um Um Um Um Um Um Um - Major Lance
Wang Dang Doodle - Koko Taylor

Who Put the Bomp - Barry Mann
Woo Hoo - Rock-a-Teens
Ya Ya - Lee Dorsey
Yakety Yak - Coasters
Zip A Dee Doo Dah - Bob B. Soxx & The Blue Jeans

Novelty Tunes

123 Redlight - 1910 Fruitgum Co
Alley Oop - Dante & The Evergreens / Hollywood Argyles
Baby Talk - Jan & Dean
Ballad of Davy Crockett - Bill Hayes
Beep Beep - Playmates
Boy Named Sue - Johnny Cash
Ding Dong the Witch is Dead - Fifth Estate
Gimme Dat Ding - Pipkins
Got a Match - Daddy-O's
Has Your Chewing Gum Lost It's Flavor - Lonnie Donegan
Juanita Banana - Peels
Junk Food Junkie - Larry Croce
King Tut - Steve Martin & Toot Uncommons
Kookie Kookie, Lend Me Your Comb - Edd Byrnes & Connie   Stevens
Leader of the Laundromat - Detergents
Long Tall Texan - Murry Kellum
Martian Hop - Ran Dells
Mr. Custer - Larry Verne
Nag - Halos
Puttin' On The Ritz - Taco
Ringo I Love You - Bonnie Jo Mason (Cher)
Roberta - Reverend Billy C. Wirtz
Seven Little Girls Sitting in the Back Seat - Paul Evans
Simon Says - 1910 Fruitgum Co
Shaving Creme - Benny Bell
Small Sad Sam - Phil Michaels
There Coming to Take Me Away - Napolean XIV (Jerry Samuels)
Tie Me Kangaroo Down Sport - Rolf Harris
The All American Boy - Bill Parsons
The Jolly Green Giant - Kingsmen
Transfusion - Nervous Norvus
Winchester Cathedral - New Vaudeville Band

Yogi - Ivy Three
Uh Oh (Parts I & II) - Nutty Squirrels

Novelty - Stan Freberg (In a Class All His Own)

John & Marsha
St. George & The Dragonet
Heartbreak Hotel
Payola Roll Blues
Green Christmas
Little Blue Riding Hood
Columbus Discovers America
Sh-Boom
The Great Pretender
I've Got You Under My Skin
Banana Boat Song
Yellow Rose of Texas
Wun'erful Wun'erful
I'm Gettin' Nuttin' for Christmas

Novelty - Ray Stevens (Ditto)

Ahab the Arab
Gitarzan
The Streak
Mississippi Squirrel Revival
Shriner's Convention
Also the straight classics: Everything is Beautiful & Turn On Your Radio

Novelty - Buchanon & Goodman (Likewise)

Flying Saucers (Parts I & II) .... #3 (1956) Mr. Jaws ....#1 (1976)
Hey E.T. .... (1983) & a ton of other Novelty Tunes like " Batman & his
Grandma " They invented & were Masters of the " Break in Record", where
other songs break into the main theme to tell a story! They spent years
in court over copyright violations. They are actually in Guinness Book
of World Records for most novelty / comedy records on the charts .

By the Numbers

1,2,3 - Len Barry (with Dovells, then went solo)
One - Three Dog Night
One Bad Apple - Osmonds
One Mint Julep - Clovers
One Bourbon, One Scotch & One Beer - Amos Milburn & His Chicken
Shackers / George Thorogood & Delaware Destroyers
One Fine Day - Chiffons
A Million to One - Jimmy Charles & The Revelettes

It Takes Two - Marvin Gaye & Kim Weston
Love Me Two Times - Doors
Two Divided By Love - Grass Roots
Love On a Two Way Street - Moments
Be My Number Two - Joe Jackson
Two Out of Three Ain't Bad - Meatloaf

Three Times a Lady - Commodores
Knock Three Times - Tony Orlando & Dawn

Let the Four Winds Blow - Fats Domino

Five O'Clock World - Vogues

From a Buick 6 - Bob Dylan
Six O'Clock News - John Prine

Seven Little Girls Sitting in the Backseat - Paul Evans
Seven Rooms of Gloom - Four Tops
Eight Miles High - Byrds
Eight Days A Week - Beatles

Riot in Cell Block #9 - Robins
Cloud 9 - Temptations
9 to 5 - Dolly Parton
Revolution #9 - Beatles

Sixteen Reasons - Connie Stevens

Edge of Seventeen - Stevie Nicks
Seventeen - Boyd Bennett (1955)

Eighteen - Alice Cooper

Hey Nineteen - Steely Dan
24 Hours from Tulsa - Gene Pitney

Forty Miles of Bad Road - Duane Eddy

98.6 - Keith

100 Pounds of Clay - Gene McDaniels

Numbers - Thousand

1000 Stars - Kathy Young & Innocents
The Night Has A 1000 Eyes - Bobby Vee
A 1000 Miles Away - Heartbeats
I Love You a 1000 Times - Platters
Land of 1000 Dances - Wilson Pickett / Cannibal & The Headhunters

Numbers - Millions & More

A Million to One - Jimmy Charles & The Revelettes
One in a Million - Platters
One in a Million You - Larry Graham
Billion Dollar Babies - Alice Cooper

One Hit Wonders of World (OHWOW #1's in boldface)

What is a **One Hit Wonder** ? Some would say *One hit in the Top 40*. My criteria: If an artist has only one hit in the Top 20 or if it didn't hit the Top 20, but is a classic song everyone knows or if it is the only song that anyone really remembers from an artist or group !!!   Take the case of poor Norman Greenbaum. He recorded tons of great songs, but.no one remembers any of them except "Spirit in the Sky " or The Royal Guardsmen - Snoopy & The Red Baron. They actually hit #15 with "The Return of the Red Baron" In my opinion, they are still a **One Hit Wonder** ! You be the judge!!!

The Fabulous 50's (One Hit Wonders)

Sh-Boom - Chords (1954)
Third Man Theme - Anton Karas (#1 -1954)

Black Denim Trousers - Cheers (1955)
Earth Angel - Penguins (1955)
It's A Sin to Tell a Lie - Something Smith & The Redheads (1955)
Let Me Go Lover Joan Weber (#1 - 1955)
Plantation Song - Lenny Dee (1955)
Seventeen - Boyd Bennett (1955)

Cindy Oh Cindy - Vince Martin & Tarriers (1956)
Goodnight My Love - Jesse Belvin (1956)
Moonglow (Theme from Picnic) - Morris Stoloff (1956)
True Love - Grace Kelly (1956)

Black Slacks - Joe Bennett & The Sparkletones (1957)
Happy Happy Birthday Baby - Tune Weavers (1957)
Little Bitty Pretty One - Thurston Harris (1957)
Marianne - Terry Gilkyson & The Easy Riders (1957)
Mr. Lee - Bobettes (1957)
Rainbow - Russ Hamilton (1957)

Baubles, Bangles, & Beads - Kirby Stone Four (1958)
Book of Love - Monotones (1958)
Chanson d'Amour - Art & Dotty Todd (1958)
Dinner with Drac - John Zacherle (1958)
Endless Sleep - Jody Reynolds (1958)
Get a Job - Silhouettes (#1 - 1958)
He's Got the Whole World in His Hands - Laurie London (1958)
Jennie Lee - Jan & Arnie (1958)
Little Star - Elegants (#1 - 1958)
One Summer Night - Danleers (1958)
Purple People Eater - Sheb Wooley (1958)
Rockin' Robin - Bobby Day (1958)
Summertime, Summertime - Jamies (1958)
To Know Him is to Love Him - Teddy Bears (with Phil Spector) (1958)
Volare - Domenico Modugno (1958)
Wishing for Your Love - Voxpoppers (1958)

Battle of Kookamonga - Homer & Jethro (1959)
Here Comes Summer - Jerry Keller (1959)
I've Had It - Bell Notes (1959)
Only You - Frank Pourcel (1959)
Sea of Love - Phil Phillips (1959)
Sorry (I Ran All the Way Home) - Impalas (1959)
Tell Him No - Travis & Bob (1959)

The Sensational 60's (One Hit Wonders)

Alley Oop - Dante & The Evergreens / **Hollywood Argyles (#1 - 1960)**
Angel Baby - Rosie & The Originals (1960)
Love You So - Ron Holden & The Thunderbirds (1960)
Let's Think About Livin' - Bob Luman (1960)
Let the Little Girl Dance - Bobby Bland (1960)
Mule Skinner Blues - Fendermen (1960)
Sandy - Larry Hall (1960)
Sailor (Your Home is the Sea) - Lolita (1960)
Yogi - Ivy Three (1960)

Baby Sittin' Boogie - Buzz Clifford (1961)
I Just Don't Understand - Ann Margaret (1961)
Kokomo - Asia Minor (1961)
Little Bit O'Soap - Jarmels (1961)
Pretty Little Angel Eyes - Curtis Lee (1961)
This Time - Troy Shondell (1961)
Who Put the Bomp - Barry Mann (1961)

Al Di La - Emilio Percoli (1962)
Close to Cathy - Mike Clifford (1962)
Dear One - Larry Finnegan (1962)
Do You Love Me - The Contours (1962)
Hey Baby - Bruce Channel (1962)
I Remember You - Frank Ifield (1962)
I Know - Barbara George (1962)
Jamie - Eddie Holland (1962)
Johnny Get Angry - Joanie Sommers (1962)
Just One Look - Doris Troy (1962)
Party Lights - Claudine Clark (1962)
Perculator (Twist) - Billy Joe & The Checkmates (1962)

Popsicles, Icicles - The Murmaids (1962)
Pop Pop Popeye - The Sherrys (1962)
Snap Your Fingers - Joe Henderson (1962)
Shout Shout (Knock Yourself Out) - Ernie Maresca (1962)
Tell Him - Exciters (1962)
Telestar - Tornadoes (1962)
What's Your Name - Don & Juan (1962)
Village of Love - Nathaniel Mayer (1962)
Wild Weekend - Rockin' Rebels (1962)
You Better Move On - Arthur Alexander (1962)
You'll Lose A Good Thing - Barbara Lynn (1962)

Cry to Me - Betty Harris (1963)
Dominique - Singing Nun (#1 - 1963)
I Wonder What She's Doing Tonight - Barry & The Tamerlanes (1963)
Killer Joe - Rocky Fellas (1963)
Mr. Bassman - Johnny Cymbal (1963)
Midnight Mary - Joe Powers (1963)
More - Kai Winding (1963)
Our Winter Love - Bill Pursell (1963)
Pipeline - Chantays (1963)
Rhythmn of the Rain - Cascades (1963)
Sally Go 'Round the Roses - Jaynetts (1963)
Swinging on a Star - Big Dee Irwin (1963)
Sukiyaki - Kyu Sakamoto (1963)
The Kind of Boy You Can't Forget - Raindrops (1963)
Wipeout - Surfaris (1963)

Girl from Ipanema - Astrud Gilberto & Stan Getz (1964)
Have I the Right - Honeycombs (1964)
Hippy Hippy Shake - Swinging Blue Jeans (1964)
I Wanna Love Him So Bad - Jellybeans (1964)
(Just Like) Romeo & Juliet - Reflections (1964)
Last Kiss - J. Frank Wilson & The Cavaliers (1964)
Rip Van Winkle - Devotions (1964)
Tobacco Road - Nashville Teens (1964)

A Walk in the Black Forest - Horst Jankowski (1965)
Baby the Rain Must Fall - Glenn Yarborough (1965)
Everyone's Gone to the Moon - Jonathon King (1965)

Goldfinger - Shirley Bassey (1965)
Keep on Dancing - The Gentrys (1965)
Liar Liar - Castaways (1965)
The Men in My Little Girl's Life - Mike Douglas (1965)
The Boy from New York City - Ad Libs (1965)
You've Got to Hide Your Love Away - Silkie (1965)

Cool Jerk - Capitols (1966)
Dirty Water - Standells (1966)
Double Shot of My Baby's Love - Swinging Medallions (1966)
Elusive Butterfly - Bob Lind (1966)
Harlem Nocturne - Viscounts (1966)
Oh How Happy - Shades of Blue (1966)
Psychotic Reaction - Count Five (1966)
They're Coming to Take Me Away - Napolean XiV (1966)
The Cheater - Bob Kuban & The In Men (1966)
Talk Talk - Music Machine (1966)

Back on the Street Again - Sunshine Company (1967)
Come On Down to My Boat - Every Mother's Son (1967)
Expressway to Your Heart - Soul Survivors (1967)
For What It's Worth - Buffalo Springfield (1967)
Green Tambourine - Lemon Pipers (1967)
I Had Too Much to Dream Last Night - Electric Prunes (1967)
Judy in Disguise (with Glasses) - John Fred & His Playboy Band (1967)
Let It All Hang Out - Hombres (1967)
Next Plane to London - The Rose Garden (1967)
Pata Pata - Miriam Makeba (1967)
Then You Can Tell Me Goodbye - Casinos (1967)
We Ain't Got Nothin' Yet - Blues Magoos (1967)
Yellow Balloon - The Yellow Balloon (1967)

A Question of Temperature - The Balloon Farm (1968)
Angel of the Morning - Merrilee Rush (1968)
Fire - The Crazy World of Arthur Brown (1968)
Harper Valley PTA - Jeannie C. Riley (1968)
In-A-Gadda-Da-Vida - Iron Butterfly - Album Cut 19 min (1968)
I Love You - People (1968)
Journey to the Center of the Mind - Amboy Dukes (Ted Nugent) (1968)
Little Arrows - Leapy Lee (1968)

Love Makes A Woman - Barbara Acklin (1968)
Master Jack - Four Jacks & A Jill (1968)
MacArthur Park - Richard Harris (1968)
More Today Than Yesterday - Spiral Staircase (1968)
Naturally Stoned - Avante Garde (1968)
Pictures of Matchstick Men - Status Quo (1968)
Reach Out of the Darkness - Friend & Lover (1968)
Summertime Blues - Blue Cheer (1968)
Shame Shame - Magic Lanterns (1968)
Smile a Little Smile for Me - Flying Machine (1968)
You Keep Me Hanging On - Vanilla Fudge (1968)

Baby It's You - Smith (1969)
Gimme Gimme Good Lovin' - Crazy Elephant (1969)
Hot Smoke & Sassafras - Bubble Puppy (1969)
In the Year 2525 - Zager & Evans (#1 - 1969)
Israelites - Desmond Decker (1969)
Kimo-Sabe - Electric Indian (1969)
Love Can Make You Happy - Mercy (1969)
Morning Girl - Neon Philharmonic (1969)
My Pledge of Love - Joe Jeffrey Group (1969)
Na Na Hey Hey Kiss Him Goodbye - Steam (1969)
Something in the Air - Thunderclap Newman (1969)
Will You Be Staying After Sunday - Peppermint Rainbow (1969)

The Swinging 70's (One Hit Wonders)

All Right Now - Free (1970)
Tighter & Tighter - Alive & Kicking (1970)
Gimme Dat Ding - Pipkins (1970)
House of the Rising Sun - Frijid Pink (1970)
In the Summertime - Mungo Jerry (1970)
Love Grows (Where My Rosemary Goes) - Edison Lighthouse (1970)
Mississippi Queen - Mountain (1970)
Montego Bay - Bobby Bloom (1970)
My Baby Loves Lovin' - White Plains (1970)
Reflections of My Life - Marmalade (1970)
Ride Captain Ride - Blues Image (1970)
Spirit in the Sky - Norman Greenbaum (1970)
Somebody's Been Sleeping - 100 Proof Aged in Soul (1970)

Sweet Mary - Wadsworth Mansion (1970)
The Rapper - Jaggerz (1970)
Venus - Shocking Blue (1970)
Are You Ready - Pacific Gas & Electric Co (1970)
Baby Take Me Iin Your Arms - Jefferson (1970)
Go Back - Crabby Appleton (1970)
Hey There Lonely Girl - Eddie Holman (1970)
Indiana Wants Me - R. Dean Taylor (1970)
Lay a Little Lovin' On Me - Robin McNamara (1970)
Ma Belle Ami - Tee Set (1970)
Ooh Oooh Child - Five Stairsteps (1970)
Rose Garden - Lynn Anderson (1970)
Vehicle - Ides of March (1970)
Yellow River - Christie (1970)

Chick-A-Boom - Daddy Dewdrop (1971)
Desiderata - Les Crane (1971)
Funky Nassau - The Beginning of the End (1971)
Help Me Make It Through The Night - Sammi Smith (1971)
Here Comes The Sun - Richie Havens (1971)
I'd Love to Change the World - Ten Years After (1971)
I've Found Someone of My Own - The Free Movement (1971)
Mr. Big Stuff - Jean Knight (1971)
Once You Understand - Think (1971)
One Toke Over the Line - Brewer & Shipley (1971)
One Tin Soldier (The Legend of Billy Jack) - Coven (1971)
Put Your Hand in the Hand - Ocean (1971)
Rings - Cymarron (1971)
Smiling Faces Sometimes - The Undisputed Truth (1971)
Stay Awhile - Bells (1971)
Timothy - Buoys (1971)
Toast & Marmalade for Tea - Tin Tin (1971)
Trapped By a Thing Called Love - Denise LaSalle (1971)

Bang a Gong (Get It On) - T-Rex (1972)
Beautiful Sunday - Daniel Boone (1972)
Convention '72 - Delegates (1972)
Gone - Joey Heatherton (1972)
Good Time Charlie's Got the Blues - Danny O'Keefe (1972)
Hocus Pocus - Focus (1972)

Hot Rod Lincoln - Commander Cody & His Lost Planet Airmen (1972)
How Do You Do - Mouth & MacNeal (1972)
Hold Your Head Up - Argent (1972)
I'd Like to Teach the World to Sing - Hillside Singers (1972)
Joy - Apollo 100 (1972)
Jungle Fever - Chakachas (1972)
Mister Can't You See - Buffy Saint-Marie (1972)
Motorcycle Mama - Sailcat (1972)
Natural High - Bloodstone (1973)Sauvecito - Malo (1972)
Oh Babe What Would You Say - Hurricane Smith (1972)
Precious & Few - Climax (1972)
Popcorn - Hot Butter (1972)
Sunshine - Jonathon Edwards (1972)
White Lies, Blue Eyes - Bullet (1972)

Brother Louie - Stories (1973)
Dancin' In The Moonlight - King Harvest (1973)
Daisy a Day - Jud Strunk (1973)
Dead Skunk - Loudon Wainwright III (1973)
Dueling Banjos - Steve Mandell & Eric Weissberg (1973)
I'm Doin' Fine Now - New York City (1973)
My Maria - B.W. Stevenson (1973)
Playground in My Mind - Clint Holmes (1973)
Soul Makossa - Manu Dibango (1973)
Smokin' In The Boys Room - Brownsville Station (1973)
Teddy Bear Song - Barbara Fairchild (1973)
The Night The Lights Went Out in Georgia - Vicki Lawrence (1973)
Wildflower - Skylark (1973)
Why Can't We Live Together - Timmy Thomas (1973)

Be Thankful for What You've Got - William DeVaughn (1974)
Erus Tu (Touch the Wind) - Mocedades (1974)
First Class - Beach Baby (1974)
Hang On In There Baby - Johnny Bristol (1974)
Hooked On a Feeling - Blue Swede (1974)
I Can Help - Billy Swan (1974)
Kung Fu Fighting - Carl Douglas (1974)
Life is a Rock (But the Radio Rolled Me) - Reunion (1974)
Last Kiss - Wednesday (1974)
Midnight at the Oasis - Maria Muldaur (1974)

Rock Your Baby - George MacRae (1974)
Rock & Roll Hoochie Coo - Rick Derringer (1974)
Rock On - David Essex (1974)
Seasons in the Sun - Terry Jacks (1974)
TSOP (The Sound of Philadelphia) - MFSB (Mother Father Sister Brother)
The Entertainer - Marvin Hamlisch (1974)
The Night Chicago Died - Paper Lace (1974)
The Americans - Byron MacGregor (1974)
Tubular Bells - Mike Oldfield (1974)
The Lord's Prayer - Sister Janet Mead (1974)
Tell Me a Lie - Sami Jo (1974)
Woman to Woman - Shirley Brown (1974)

Autobahn - Kraftwerk (1975)
Chevy Van - Sammy Johns (1975)
Dynomite - Bazuka (1975)
Feelings - Morris Albert (1975)
How Long - Ace (1975)
I'm Not Lisa - Jesse Colter (1975)
Lovin' You - Minnie Riperton (1975)
Magic - Pilot (1975)
Never Been Any Reason - Head East (1975)
Rockin' Chair - Gwen McCrae (1975)
Sad Sweet Dreamer - Soul Sensation (1975)
Shaving Cream - Benny Bell (1975)
The Hustle - Van McCoy (1975)

Afternoon Delight - Starlight Vocal Band (1976)
Disco Duck - Rick Dees (1976)
Fifth of Beethoven - Walter Murphy & The Big Apple Band (1976)
Fooled Around & Fell in Love - Elvin Bishop (1976)
Get Dancin' - Disco Tex (Monty Rock III) & The Sexolettes (1976)
Happy Days - Pratt & McClain (1976)
Junk Food Junkie - Larry Croce (1976)
Movim' - Brass Construction (1976)
Making Our Dreams Come True - Cyndi Grecco (1976)
Play That Funky Music - Wild Cherry (1976)
Turn the Beat Around - Vicki Sue Robinson (1976)
The Boys Are Back in Town - Thin Lizzy (1976)
Union Man - Cale Brothers (1976)

Wham Bam - Silver (1976)

Ariel - Dean Freidman (1977)
Black Betty - Ram Jam (1977)
Dancin' Man - Q (1977)
Don't Give Up on Us - David Soul (1977)
Don't Leave Me This Way - Thelma Houston (1977)
Float On - Floaters (1977)
Heavan on the 7th Floor - Paul Nicholas (1977)
Jeans On - David Dundas (1977)
Mah Na Mah Na - Piero Umiliani (1977)
Native New Yorker - Odessey (1977)
Smoke from a Distant Fire - Sanford Townsend Band (1977)
Trying to Love Two - William Bell (1977)
Telephone Man - Meri Wilson (1977)
You Light Up My Life - Debby Boone (1977)

Because the Night - Patti Smith Group (1978)
Dance Across the Floor - Jimmy Horn (1978)
Emotion - Samantha Sang (1978)
Falling - LeBlanc & Carr (1978)
Get Off - Foxy (1978)
Hot Child in the City - Nick Gilder (1978)
I Love The Nightlife (Disco 'Round) - Alicia Bridges (1978)
I Can't Stand the Rain - Eruption (1978)
I'm Gonna Take Care of Everything - Rubicon (1978)
King Tut - Steve Martin & The Tut Uncommons (1978)
Love is in the Aair - John Paul Young (1978)
Magnet & Steel - Walter Egan (1978)
Ring My Bell - Anita Ward (1978)
Rivers of Babylon - Boney M (1978)
Undercover Angel - Alan O'Day (1978)

Born to Be Alive - Patrick Hernandez (1979)
Cruel to Be Kind - Nick Lowe (1979)
Driver's Seat - Sniff N' The Tears (1979)
Get Used to It - Roger Voudouris (1979)
Hold On - Ian Gomm (1979)
I Got My Mind Made Up (You Can't Get It Girl) - Instant Funk (1979)
I Don't Like Mondays - Boomtown Rats (Bob Geldof) (1979)

Just When I Needed You Most - Randy Vanwarmer (1979)
Knock on Wood - Amii Stewart (1979)
Makin' It - David Naughton (1979)
Pop Musik - M (1979)
Video Killed the Radio Star - Buggles (1979
What You Won't Do for Love - Bobby Caldwell (1979)

One Hit Wonders (Artists Special Mention)

Tony Burrows - Session Vocalist

Love Grows (Where My Rosemary Goes) - Edison Lighthouse
My Baby Loves Lovin' - White Plains
Gimme Dat Ding - Pipkins
United We Stand - Brotherhood of Man

Ron Dante (Carmine Granito)

Archies - Sugar Sugar
Cuff Links - Tracy
Detergents - Leader of the Laundromat

Gary Paxton

Cherry Pie - Skip & Flip
Alley Oop - Hollywood Argyles (Sandy Nelson on drums)

Sonny Gerace

Time Won't Let Me - Outsiders
Precious & Few - Climax

Johnny Cymbal

Mr. Bass Man - Johnny Cymbal
98.6 - Derek

Bobby Darin

Early in the Morning - Rinky Dinks

Four Seasons

Don't Think Twice It's All Right - Wonder Who

All by the Same Group (Moonlighting ... Can you say "Contract")

Peanut Butter - Marathons
Stranded in the Jungle - Jayhawks
Watusi - Vibrations

Originals, Remakes, & Covers

Covers are Songs that are released at the same time by different artists & they compete with one another. Often done in the early days of Rock & Roll. A *black* artist would release a record & it would be " covered " by a *white* artist. An example Fats Domino - Ain't That a Shame was covered by Pat Boone. They were released at the same time & were "hits" for both artists.

Remakes are recordings of the same song by different artists that are not competing. They are released after the original has run it's course. As example Carl Perkins - Blue Suede Shoes remade by Elvis after Carl's Record left the charts. Carl said that that was the nicest thing anyone had ever done for him!

Originals are recordings that were made by one artist & didn't go very far, then remade by another artist that had a big hit with the song. An example would be Nobody But Me - Isley Brothers & the # 1 hit by the Human Beinz.

Act Naturally - Buck Owens ~ Ringo Starr
Baby I Need Your Lovin' - Four Tops ~ Johnny Rivers
Bad to Me - Billy Joe Royal & Dakotas ~ Beatles
Barbara Ann - Regents ~ Beach Boys
Black Magic Woman - Fleetwood Mac ~ Santana
Blue Monday - Smiley Lewis ~ Fats Domino
C.C. Ryder - Chuck Willis ~ Mitch Ryder & Detroit Wheels
Close Your Eyes - Five Keys ~ Peaches & Herb
Dedicated to the One I Love - Five Royales ~ Shirelles ~ Mamas & Papas
Do Wah Diddy - Exciters ~ Manfred Mann
Everlasting Love - Robert John ~ Carl Carlton
Earth Angel - Penquins ~ Crew Cuts
Feels So Good - Johnny Preston ~ Shirley & Lee ~ Bunny Sigler

Good Lovin' - Clovers ~ Olympics ~ Rascals
Handy Man - Jimmy Jones ~ James Taylor
Hound Dog - Big Mama Thornton ~ Elvis
Hippy Hippy Shake - Chan Romero ~ Swinging Blue Jeans
Hurt So Bad - Little Anthony & Imperials ~ Linda Ronstadt
I Feel So Bad - Chuck Willis ~ Elvis
I Hear You Knockin' - Smiley Lewis ~ Gail Storm
I Heard It Through The Grapevine - Gladys Knight & The Pips
~ Marvin Gaye ~ CCR
I'm Leavin' It All Up to You - Don & Dewey ~ Dale & Grace
I'm Walkin' - Fats Domino ~ Ricky Nelson
Land of 1000 Dances - Wilson Pickett ~ Cannibal & The Headhunters
Little Darlin' - Gladiolas ~ Diamonds
Locomotion - Little Eva ~ Grand Funk Railroad
Mockingbird - Inez & Charles Fox ~ Carly Simon
Money (That's What I Want) - Barrett Strong ~ Kingsmen ~ Beatles
Mountain of Love - Harold Dorman ~ Johnny Rivers
My Girl Sloopy - The Vibrations ~ Hang on Sloopy - McCoys
Needles & Pins - Jackie DeShannon ~ Searchers
Nobody But Me - Isley Brothers ~ Human Beinz
Not Fade Away - Buddy Holly ~ Rolling Stones
One Night of Sin - Smiley Lewis ~ One Night with You - Elvis
Piece of My Heart - Irma Franklin ~ Janis Joplin
Ruby Baby - Drifters ~ Dion
Runaway - Del Shannon ~ Bonnie Raitt
Sh-Boom - Chords ~ Crew Cuts
Shake A Tail Feather - Five Du-Tones ~ James & Bobby Purify
Silhouettes - Rays ~ Diamonds
Such a Night - Bunny Paul ~ Drifters ~ Elvis
Time Is On My Side - Irma Thomas ~ Rolling Stones
Twist - Hank Ballard & the Midnighters ~ Chubby Checker
Unchained Melody - Les Baxter ~ Vito & Salutations ~ Righteous Brothers
Word of Love - Buddy Holly ~ Mamas & Papas
You Belong to Me - Jo Stafford ~ Duprees

Pat Boone (Charles Eugene Patrick Boone)

When Rock & Roll was viewed as evil & the work of Satan, he covered many
of the black artists " Race " music hits in the early days & made them
acceptable to his white bread audiences! Pat Boone had 38 Top 40 Hits.

Ain't that A Shame - Fats Domino (Million Seller for both.........
Fats Domino at #16 & Pat Boone at #2)
Tutti Fruiti - Little Richard
Crazy Little Mama (At My Front Door) - El Dorados (#7 - 1957)
I'll Be Home - Flamingos
I Almost Lost My Mind - Ivory Joe Hunter

Linda Ronstadt

Hurt So Bad - Little Anthony & Imperials
Back in the USA - Chuck Berry
Your No Good - Betty Everett
Ooh Baby Baby - Smokey Robinson & Miracles
That'll Be The Day - Buddy Holly
Tumbling Dice - Rolling Stones
When Will I Be Loved - Everly Brothers
Heatwave - Martha & The Vandellas

Parks

Itchycoo Park - Small Faces
MacArthur Park - Richard Harris / Four Tops
Palisades Park - Freddie Cannon
Rain, Park, & Other Things - Cowsills
Sitting in the Park - Billy Stewart
Saturday in the Park - Chicago

Party Tunes

Ain't Nothin' But a House Party - Showstoppers / J. Geils
Havin' a Party - Sam Cooke / Southside Johnny & The Asbury Jukes
It's My Party - Leslie Gore
Let's Have a Party - Wanda Jackson
Party Lights - Claudine Clark
Party All The Time - Eddie Murphy
Party Doll - Buddy Knox
Party - Elvis
Rock & Roll Party Party Queen - Louis St. Louis
Splish Splash - Bobby Darin
You've Got to Fight (For Your Right to Party) - Beastie Boys

Patriotic

America the Beautiful - Ray Charles
Born in the USA - Bruce Springsteen
God Bless America - Kate Smith / Connie Francis
Pledge of Allegiance - Red Skelton
Pledge of Alligiance - Red Skelton / John Wayne
The Americans - Gordon Sinclair (A Canadian's Opinion)

Pets

Bunny Hop - Ray Anthony / Traditional
White Rabbit - Jefferson Airplane

See Ya Later Alligator - Bill Haley & His Comets
Crocodile Rock - Elton John

Monkey Time - Major Lance
Mickey's Monkey - Smokey Robinson & The Miracles

Crawlin' King Snake Blues - John Lee Hooker
Spiders & Snakes - Jim Stafford
Tubesnake Boogie - ZZ Top

Tiger - Fabian
Eye of the Tiger - Survivor

Cattle Call - Eddy Arnold
Dead Skunk - London Wainwright III
Joy to the World - Three Dog Night (Bullfrog)
Muskrat Love - Captain & Tennile
The Lion Sleeps Tonight - Tokens

& Birds

And Your Bird Can Sing - Beatles
Baby I Love Your Way / Freebird (Free Baby) - Will to Power
Big Bird - Eddie Floyd
Bluebirds Over the Mountain - Ersel Hickey
Birds & The Bees - Jewel Aikens

Bird is the Word - Rivingtons
Blackbird - Beatles
Chicken Shack Boogie - Amos Wilburn
Dixie Chicken - Little Feat
Freebird - Lynyrd Skynyrd
Fly Like An Eagle - Steve Miller Band
Free As a Bird - Beatles
Little Red Rooster - Howlin' Wolf
Mockingbird - Inez Foxx / Carly Simon & James Taylor
Norwegian Wood (This Bird Has Flown) - Beatles
Rockin' Robin - Bobby Day
Shake A Tail Feather - Five Du-Tones / James & Bobby Purify /
Mitch Ryder & the Detroit Wheels
Surfin' Bird - Trashmen / Pee Wee Herman

& Butterflies Are Free

Butterfly - Charlie Gracie
Elusive Butterfly - Bob Lind
Butterfly Kisses - Bob Carlyle
Dog & Butterfly - Heart

& Cats   (Also See Pets - Lions & Tigers)

Alley Cat - Bent Fabric / Bobby Rydell (with words ?!?)
Alley Cat (Speed Up Version) - Traditional
Bear Cat - Rufus Thomas
Cat Scratch Fever - Ted Nugent
Honky Cat - Elton John
Leave My Kitten Alone - Little Willie John / Beatles
Look What The Cat Dragged In - Poisin
Nashville Cats - Lovin' Spoonful
Three Cool Cats - Beatles
Stray Cat Strut - Stray Cats
What's New Pussycat - Tom Jones
Year of the Cat - Al Stewart

& Dogs

Atomic Dog - George Clinton

Bird Dog - Everly Brothers
Diamond Dogs - David Bowie
Dog & Butterfly - Heart
Gonna Buy Me a Dog - Monkees
Giving the Dog a Bone - AC /DC
Hair of the Dog - Nazareth
Hound Dog - Big Mama Thornton / Elvis
How Much is that Doggie in the Window - Patti Page
Hound Dog Man - Fabian (Forte)
I'll Be Doggone - Marvin Gaye
Jackie Wilson - Doggin' Around
Me & You & a Dog Named Boo - Lobo
Puppy Love - Paul Anka
Walking the Dog - Rufus Thomas
Wouldn't Treat a Dog, the Way You Treated Me - Bobby Bland

& Horses

A Horse with No Name - America
Chestnut Mare - Byrds
El Paso - Marty Robbins
Horse - Cliff Nobles & Co
Midnight Rider - Allman Brothers
Mustang Sally - Wilson Pickett
Night Rider - Elvis
On a Carousel - Hollies
One Trick Pony - Paul Simon
Pony Time - Chubby Checker
Ride Your Pony - Lee Dorsey
Ride Like The Wind - Christopher Cross
Riders on the Storm - Doors
Wild Horses - Rolling Stones
Wildfire - Michael Martin Murphey

Private Eyes

I Can See for Miles - Who
Magnum P.I. - Mike Post
Peter Gunn - Duane Eddy
Private Eyes - Hall & Oates

Shaft - Isaac Hayes
Theme from Dragnet - Ray Anthony
Watching the Detectives - Elvis Costello

Psychedelic Sixties (Some Songs That Defined It for Me At Least)

A Day in the Life - Beatles
All Along the Watchtower - Bob Dylan / Jimi Hendrix
Eight Miles High - Byrds
Eve of Destruction - Barry MaGuire
For What It's Worth - Buffalo Springfield
Fortunate Son - CCR
Get Together - Youngbloods
I Am the Walrus - Beatles
In-A-Gadda-Da-Vida - Iron Butterfly (Yes, the 19 min album cut)
Incense & Peppermints - Strawberry Alarm Clock
I Can See for Miles - Who
Journey to the Center of Your Mind - Amboy Dukes
Like a Rolling Stone - Bob Dylan
Light My Fire - Doors
Magical Mystery Tour - Beatles
Purple Haze - Jimi Hendrix Experience
Sgt, Pepper's Lonely Hearts Club Band - Beatles
Somebody to Love - Jefferson Airplane
Sunshine of Your Love - Cream
Time Has Come Today - Chambers Brothers
We've Got To Get Out of this Place - Animals
White Rabbit - Jefferson Airplane
You Keep Me Hangin' On - Vanilla Fudge

Rich

Eat The Rich - Aerosmith
First I Look at the Purse - Contours
Rich Girl - Hall & Oates

& Poor

A Poor Man's Roses (Or a Rich Man's Gold) - Patsy Cline
Ain't Got No Home - Clarence " Frogman " Henry

Down in the Boondocks - Billy Joe Royal (1965)
Gypsy Woman (She's Homeless) - Crystal Waters
Leader of the Laundromat - Detergents
Patches - Clarence Carter
Poor Side of Town - Johnny Rivers

River

Cry Me a River - Joe Cocker
Green River - CCR
Lazy River - Mills Brothers
Moody River - Pat Boone
Ol' Man River - Temptations
Red River Rock - Johnny & The Hurrcanes
River Deep, Mountain High - Four Tops & Supremes
Running Bear - Johnny Preston
Take Me to the River - Syl Johnson / Commitments
The River - Bruce Springsteen
Yellow River - Christie

Rock & Roll

Good Old Rock & Roll - Cat Mother & The All Night News Boys
Hang Up My Rock & Roll Shoes - Chuck Willis
Heart of Rock & Roll - Huey Lewis & The News
I Dig Rock & Roll Music - Peter, Paul, & Mary
It's Only Rock & Roll - Rolling Stones
It's Still Rock & Roll to Me - Billy Joel
I Love Rock & Roll - Joan Jett & The Blackhearts
Just a Singer in a Rock & Roll Band - Moody Blues
Let It Rock - Chuck Berry
Life is a Rock, But the Radio Rolled Me - Reunion (1974)
Old Time Rock & Roll - Bob Seger
R.O.C.K. in the USA - John Cougar Mellencamp
Rock & Roll - Velvet Underground
Rock & Roll Part II - Gary Glitter
Rock & Roll All Night - Kiss
Rock & Roll is King - Richie Valens
Rock & Roll is Here to Stay - Danny & The Juniors
Rock & Roll Fantasy - Bad Company

Rock & Roll Heaven - Righteous Brothers
Rock & Roll Hoochie Coo - Rick Derringer
Rock & Roll Music - Chuck Berry / Beatles / Beach Boys
Rock & Roll Party Queen - Louis St. Louis (Grease)
Rock & Roll Stew - Traffic
Rock & Roll Waltz - Kay Starr
Rock On - David Essex (1974)
Rock This Town - Stray Cats
Sweet Little Rock & Roller - Chuck Berry
So You Wanna Be a Rock & Roll Star - Byrds

Royalty

Caribbean Queen (No More Love on the Run) - Billy Ocean
Dancing Queen - ABBA
God Save the Queen - Sex Pistols
Her Royal Majesty - James Darren
Killer Queen - Queen
Little Queenie - Chuck Berry
Mississippi Queen - Mountain
Queen of the Hop - Bobby Darin
Queen of Hearts - Juice Newton
Queen of the Slipstream - Van Morrison
Queen of the Night - Whitney Houston
Rock & Roll Party Queen - Louis St. Louis (Grease Snd Trk)
Witch Queen of New Orleans - Redbone

Duke of Earl - Gene Chandler

I'm Henry VIII I Am - Herman's Hermits
King of the Road - Roger Miller
King of Pain - Police
King for Day - Thompson Twins
King Without a Queen - Dion & Del Satins

Sad

Fa Fa Fa Fa Fa Fa (Sad Song) - Otis Redding
Little Boy Sad - Johnny Burnette
Mr. Dieingly Sad - Critters

Sad Cafe - Eagles
Sad Story - Jack Scott
Sad Souvenirs - Four Tops
Sad Movies (Make Me Cry) - Sue Thompson
Sad Eyes - Robert John
Sad Sweet Dreamer - Sweet Sensation
So Sad to Watch Good Love Go Bad - Everly Brothers
Sad Mood - Sam Cooke
Sad Lisa - Cat Stevens
Sad Songs Say So Much - Elton John
Small Sad Sam - Phil Michaels
There will be Sad Songs to Make You Cry - Billy Ocean
Why Does Love Got to Be So Sad - Derek & The Dominoes

Sailing

A Pirate Looks at Forty - Jimmy Buffet
Banana Boat Song - Harry Belafonte
Catch the Wind - Donovan
Come Sail Away - Styx
Island Girl - Elton John
Red Sails in the Sunset - Platters
Ride Captain Ride - Blues Image
Sailing - Christopher Cross
Sail On - Commodores / Lionel Richie
Sailing the Wind - Loggins & Messina
Sloop John B - Beach Boys
Smooth Sailing Tonight - Isley Brothers
Son of a Son of a Sailor - Jimmy Buffet
Sail Away - Randy Newman
Sail Away - Temptations
Wooden Ships - Crosby, Stills, & Nash

School

Be True to Your School - Beach Boys
Beauty School Dropout - Frankie Avalon (Grease Snd Trk)
Catholic School Girls Rule - Red Hot Chili Peppers
Good Morning Little School Girl - John Lee Hooker / Eric Clapton / Others
Harper Valley PTA - Jeannie C. Riley

High School Confidential - Jerry Lee Lewis
Hot for Teacher - Van Halen
Rock & Roll High School - Ramones
School is Out - Gary US Bonds
School's Out - Alice Cooper
School Days - Chuck Berry
Waitin' in School - Ricky Nelson

Sea Songs

(Sitting on the) Dock of the Bay - Otis Redding
Harbour Lights - Platters
Ebb Tide - Righteous Brothers
Sea Cruise - Frankie Ford
Sea of Love - Phil Phillips / Honeydrippers
Too Many Fish in the Sea - Marvelettes
Wreck of the Edmund Fitzgerald - Gordon Lightfoot

Second Oldest Profession (or Wannabes)

Bad Girls - Donna Summer
Honky Tonk Women - Rolling Stones
Hotel California - Eagles
House of the Rising Sun - Animals / Frijid Pink
Jenny (867-5309) - Tommy Tutone
Lady Marmalade - La Belle (Patti LaBelle)
Long Tall Sally - Little RichardNutbush City Limits - Tina Turner
Painted Ladies - Ian Thomas
Roxanne - PoliceSugar Shack - Jimmy Gilmer & Fireballs
Super Freak - Rick James
Sundown - Gordon Lightfoot

Shoes

Betty Lou's Got a New Pair of Shoes - Bobby Freeman
Blue Suede Shoes - Carl Perkins / Elvis Presley
Diamonds on the Soles of Her Shoes - Paul Simon
Hang Up My Rock & Roll Shoes - Chuck Willis
Goody Two Shoes - Adam Ant
High Heel Sneakers - Tommy Tucker

Old Brown Shoe - Beatles
Pink Shoe Laces - Dodie Stevens
Sand in My Shoes - Drifters
Shoe Shine Boy - Eddie Kendricks
Walk a Mile in My Shoes - Joe South

Slow Jams

A Million to One - Jimmy Charles & Revelettes
At Last - Billie Holiday / Etta James
Always & Forever - Heat Wave
Always on My Mind - Willie Nelson / Elvis
After the Lovin' - Engelbert Humperdinck
Almost Paradise - Mike Reno & Ann Wilson
At This Moment - Billy Vera & The Beaters

Bring It On Home to Me - Sam Cooke / Animals
Break It to Me Gently - Brenda Lee

Chapel of Love- Dixie Cups
Crazy - Patsy Cline (written by Willie Nelson)
Cherish - Association
Cry - Johnnie Ray
Cherish - Kool & The Gang
Can't Help Falling in Love - Elvis
Chances Are - Johnny Mathis
Colour My World- Chicago
Can't Fight This Feeling - REO Speedwagon
Could This Be Magic - Dubs

Ebb Tide - Righteous Brothers
Emotions - Brenda Lee
Endless Love - Diana Ross & Lionel Richie
Earth Angel - Penquins
Everytime You Go Away - Paul Young

Feelings - Morris Alpert
For the Good Times - Ray Price
Feels Like The First Time - Foreigner

Harbour Lights - Platters
Have You Heard - Duprees
Hold Me, Thrill Me, Kiss Me - Mel Carter

I Want to Be Wanted - Brenda Lee
In the Still of the Nite - Five Satins
Image of a Girl - Safaris
Into the Night - Benny Mardones
I Left My Heart in San Francisco - Tony Bennett
I Swear - Skyliners
I Only Have Eyes for You - Flamingos
I'm Sorry - Brenda Lee \ Connie Francis
It's All in the Game - Tommy Edwards

Lady - Kenny Rogers
Lady in Red - Chris DeBurgh
Lovers Never Say Goodbye - Flamingos

My Girl - Temptations
My Way - Frank Sinatra / Elvis
My Prayer - Platters
Mio Amore (My Love Til the End of Time) - Flamingos
Missing You - Paul Young

One in a Million You - Larry Graham
Ooh Baby Baby - Smokey Robinson & The Miracles
Only You - Platters
One Summer Night - Danleers

Ribbon in the Sky - Stevie Wonder

Strangers in the Night - Frank Sinatra
Since I don't Have You - Skyliners
Stardust -Tommy Dorsey / Artie Shaw / Billy Ward & Dominoes
Soul & Inspiration - Righteous Brothers
Surfer Girl- Beach Boys
Smoke Gets in Your Eyes - Platters

The Great Pretender - Platters
Truly- Lionel Richie

Tonight I Celebrate My Love - Peabo Bryson & Roberta Flack
Three Times a Lady - Commodores
This Time - Troy Shondell
Tell It Like It Is - Aaron Neville
That's What Friend's Are For - Dionne Warwick & Friends
The Greatest Love of All - Whitney Houston / George Benson
Twilight Time - Platters
Take Time to Know Her - Percy Sledge

Unchained Melody - Righteous Brothers
Unforgetable - Nat "King" Cole & Natalie Cole
When A Man Loves a Woman - Percy Sledge / Michael Bolton
Wonderful Tonight - Eric Clapton
Whiter Shade of Pale - Procul Harem
What a Wonderful World - Louis Armstrong
Wind Beneath My Wings - Bette Midler
What Becomes of the Broken Hearted - Jimmy Ruffin
Wishing on a Star - Rose Royce / Cover Girls
What's Your Name - Don & Juan
When a Man Loves a Woman - Percy Sledge

You Were Mine - Fireflies
You Belong to Me - Jo Stafford / Duprees
You've Lost That Lovin' Feeling - Righteous Brothers

Soul

Agent Double O Soul - Edwin Starr
Heart & Soul - Cleftones
Heart Full of Soul - Yardbirds
Hot Patootie, Bless My Soul - Rocky Horror Picture Show
Little Bit O' Soul - Music Explosion
Memphis Soul Stew - King Curtis
Mr. Soul - Neil Young
Soul Man - Sam & Dave / Blues Brothers
Soul Twist - King Curtis
Soul Finger - Bar Kays
Soul Deep - Box Tops
Soul & Inspiration - Righteous Brothers
Soulful Strut - Youngholt Unlimited

Stone Soul Picnic - Fifth Dimension
Sweet Soul Music - Arthur Connelly / Sam & Dave
We Got More Soul - Dyke & The Blazers

Spaced Out

2000 Light Years from Home - Rolling Stones
Across the Universe - Beatles
Earth Angel - Penguins
Flying Saucers (Part I & II) - Buchannon & Goodman
Flying Saucers Rock & Roll - Billy Lee Riley
Lucy in the Sky with Diamonds - Beatles
Major Tom (Coming Home) - Peter Schilling
Martian Hop - Ran Dells
Mr. Spaceman - Byrds
Purple People Eater - Sheb Wooley
Rocket Man - Elton John
Santa & The Satellite - Dickie Goodman
Space Oddity - David Bowie
Space Truckin' - Deep Purple
Space Intro - Steve Miller Band
Space Cowboy - Steve Miller Band
Space Guitar - Young John Watson
Starship Trooper - Yes
Theme from Starwars - John Williams / Meco
Third Stone from the Sun - Jimi Hendrix
Telstar - Tornadoes
Thus Sprach Zarathustra (2001 Space Odessey)
Ziggy Stardust - David Bowie

Star Songs

1000 Stars - Kathy Young & The Innocents
Count Every Star - Rivieras
Good Morning Starshine - Oliver
I Told Every Little Star - Linda Scott
Little Star - Elegants (1958)
Lucky Star - Madonna
Swinging on a Star - Big Dee Irwin
Shining Star - Manhattans

Shining Star - Earth, Wind & Fire
Shooting Star - Bad Co
Star Wars Theme - Meco
Wishing on a Star - Rose Royce
When You Wish Upon a Star - Little Anthony & The Imperials
You Don't Have to be a Star to Be in My Show - Billy Davis & Marilyn McCoo

Spelling Lesson

ABC - Jackson Five
B-A-B-Y - Carla Thomas
D-I-V-O-R-C-E - Tammy Wynette
L-OV-E (Love) - Al Green
R-E-S-P-E-C-T - Otis Redding / Aretha Franklin
R-O-C-K in the USA - John Cougar Mellencamp
S-O-S - Abba
T-N-T - AC / DC
W-W-E-D (What Would Elvis Do ?) - Rev. Billy C. Wirtz
W-O-M-A-N - Etta James

States (United or Otherwise)

Sweet Home Alabama - Lynyrd Skynyrd

North to Alaska - Johnny Horton

California - Joni Mitchell
California Girls - Beach Boys
California Dreaming - Mamas & Papas

Georgia on My Mind - Ray Charles
Rainy Night in Georgia - Brook Benton

Blue Hawaii - Elvis

Private Idaho - B-52s
Indiana Wants Me - R. Dean Taylor

Kentucky Woman - Deep Purple / Elvis

Massachusettes - Bee Gees

Mississippi - John Phillips

Nebraska - Bruce Springsteen

Ohio - Crosby, Stills, Nash, & Young

Summer Songs

A Summer Song - Chad & Jeremy
Beach Baby - First Class
Brown Eyed Girl - Van Morrison
Farewell My Summer Love - Michael Jackson
Hot Fun in the Summertime - Sly & The Family Stone (1969)
Cruel Summer - Bananarama (1984)
Dancing in the Streets - Martha Reeves & The Vandellas (1964)
Endless Summer Nights - Richard Marx (1988)
Hazy Crazy Days of Summer - Nat "King" Cole (1963)
Heatwave - Martha Reeves & The Vandellas
Here Comes Summer - Jerry Keller (1959)
In the Summertime - Mungo Jerry (1970)
Sealed with A Kiss - Brian Hyland (1962)
One Summer Night - Danleers (1958)
Save Your Heart for Me - Gary Lewis & The Playboys (1965
See You in September - Happenings (1966)
Summertime Summertime - Jamies (1958)
Summer in the City - Lovin' Spoonful (1966)
Summer of 69 - Bryan Adams
Summer Love - John Travolta / Olivia Newton John
Summer Wind - Frank Sinatra (1966)
Summer Breeze - Seals & Crofts (1972)
Summer Rain - Johnny Rivers
Summertime Blues- Eddie Cochran
Summertime - Sam Cooke / Billy Stewart (1966)
Summer - War - (1976)
Summer Nights - John Travolta & Olivia Newton John (Grease) (1978)
Theme from " A Summer Place " - Percy Faith (1960)
Vacation - Connie Francis
Wonderful Summer - Robin Ward

Surfin' Songs

Bustin' Surfboards - Tornadoes
Catch a Wave - Beach Boys
Lonely Surfer - Jack Nitzsche
Louie Louie (Surfin' Louie) - Shockwaves
New York's a Lonely Town - Tradewinds
Surf City- Jan & Dean
Surf Rider - Lively Ones (Pulp Fiction)
Surf's Up - Beach Boys
Surfin' Safari - Beach Boys
Surfer Girl - Beach Boys
Surfin' Bird - Trashmen
Surfin' USA - Beach Boys
Wipe Out - Surfaris

Sweet Sixteen

Only Sixteen - Sam Cooke
Sixteen Candles - Crests
Sixteen Reasons - Connie Stevens
Sixteen Tons - Tennesee Ernie Ford
Sweet Little Sixteen - Chuck Berry
Sweet Sixteen (Part I) - B.B. King
Your Sixteen - Johnny Burnette / Ringo Starr

Sweet Tooth & Snacks

Candy Girl - Four Seasons
Candy - Big Maybelle
Cherry Pie - Marvin & Johnny / Skip & Flip
Coconut - Nilsson
Ice Cream Man - Van Halen
I Want Candy - Strangeloves
Incense & Peppermints - Strawberry Alarm Clock
Jam Up & Jelly Tight - Tommy Roe
Jellie Bellie Nellie - Larry Williams
My Boy Lollipop - Little Millie Small
Peanuts - Little Joe & The Thrillers
Peanut Butter - Marathons

Popcicles, Icicles - Murmaids
Sugar Sugar - Archies
Sugartime - McGuire Sisters
Tutti Fruiti - Little Richard
Wild Honey - Beach Boys
Wild Mountain Honey - Steve Miller Band

Tears

96 Tears - ? & The Mysterians (? was Rudy Martinez)
As Tears Go By - Rolling Stones
Drown in My Own Tears - Ray Charles
I Count the Tears - Drifters
I Cried a Tear - LaVern Baker
Lonely Teardrops - Jackie Wilson
Tears of a Clown - Smokey Robinson
Tears on My Pillow - Little Anthony & The Imperials
Teardrops - Lee Andrews & Hearts
Teardrops on Your Letter - Hank Ballard & The Midnighters
The Tracks of My Tears - Smokey Robinson

Teen Idols (Guys)

Bobby Darin (Walden Robert Cassotto)
Bobby Rydell (Robert Louis Ryderelli)
Brian Hyland
David Cassidy
Donnie Osmond
Eddie Hodges
Elvis
Fabian (Forte)
Frankie Avalon (Avalone)
Frank Sinatra
James Darren
Jimmy Clanton
Johnny Tillotson
Johnny Ray
Neil Sedaka
Paul Anka
Paul Petersen

Pat Boone
Ricky Nelson
Tab Hunter

Teen Idols (Gals)

Annette (Funicello)
Aretha Franklin
Brenda Lee
Connie Francis (Concetta Rosa Maria Franconero from Newark, NJ)
Connie Stevens
Diana Ross
Leslie Gore
Little Peggy March

Telephone #'s

Pennsylvania 6-5000 - Glenn Miller Orchestra
Jenny (867-5209) - Tommy Tutone (1982)
Beechwood 4-5789 - Marvelettes (1962)
634-5789 (Soulsville USA) - Wilson Pickett (1966)
Telephone Man - Meri Wilson
Telephone Line - ELO

The Day The Music Died (February 03, 1959)

Buddy Holly, Richie Valens & The Big Bopper were killed when their
plane went down in an Iowa cornfield minutes after take off from the
Mason City Airport.. They had been appearing at the Surf Ballroom in
Clear Lake, Iowa as part of the General Artist's Corporation " Winter
Dance Party Tour - The Biggest Show of Stars of 1959 " covering 24
Midwestern Cities. The tour bus was ill equipped for the cold Winter
weather & ther heater broke after the tour began. Waylon Jennings,
who later went on to be a Country Superstar, then a member of Buddy
Holly's band narrowly missed going on the plane. He gave up his place
to Big Bopper, who was sick & had the flu. Rumor has it they flipped a
coin. A bizarre twist of fate. The pilot, Roger Peterson, was also killed.

The Artists:

Buddy Holly (Charles Hardin Holley ~ September 7, 1936)

Peggy Sue - Buddy Holly
That'll Be the Day - Buddy Holly
Early in the Morning - Buddy Holly
That's My Desire - Buddy Holly
I'm Gonna Love You Too - Buddy Holly
Not Fade Away - Buddy Holly
Heartbeat - Buddy Holly
Rave On - Buddy Holly
Rockin' Around with Ollie Vee - Buddy Holly

Richie Valens (Richie Valensuela ~ May 13, 1941)

Come On Let's Go - Richie Valens
La Bamba - Richie Valens
Oh Donna - Richie Valens
Rock & Roll is King - Richie Valens

The Big Bopper (Jiles Perry Richardson ~ October 24, 1930)

Chantilly Lace - Big Bopper
White Lightning - Big Bopper

Frank Sardo (Billed as An Extra Added Attraction)

Fake Out - Frankie Sardo (Miss Listed on Poster as "Take Out")

Dion & Belmonts (Dion DiMucci)

I Wonder Why - Dion & The Belmonts (May 1958)
No One Knows - Dion & The Belmonts (Sept 1958)
Don't Pity Me - Dion & The Belmonts (Jan 1959)

Artists that Replaced Them on the Tour After the Crash:

Bobby Vee & The Shadows (Local Midwestern High School Band)

Frankie Avalon (Avalone)

Dede Dinah - Frankie Avalon (Jan 1958)
Ginger Bread - Frankie Avalon (July 1958)
I'll Wait for You - Frankie Avalon (Nov 1958)

Jimmy Clanton

Just a Dream - Jimmy Clanton (July 1958)
A Letter to an Angel - Jimmy Clanton (Nov 1958)
A Part of Me - Jimmy Clanton (Dec 1958)

Tribute Songs

American Pie - Don McLean
Three Stars - Tommy Dee / Eddie Cochran
Tribute to Buddy Holly - Mike Berry

<u>Time</u>

25 or 6 to 4 - Chicago
Bad Time - Grand FunkD
Didn't I (Blow Your Mind This Time) - Delfonics
Do It to Me One More Time - Captain & Tennile
Does Anybody Really Know What Time It Is ? - Chicago
Every Time I Turn Around) Back in Love Again - LTD
Finger Poppin' Time - Hank Ballard & The Midnighters
First Time I Met the Blues - Buddy Guy
Feels Like The First Time - Foreigner
Funny How Time Slips Away - Supremes
Get to the World on Time - Electric Prunes
Give Me Just a Little More Time - Chairman of the Board
Gonna Have a Funky Good Time - James Brown
Haven't Got Time for the Pain - Carly Simon
High Time We Went - Joe Cocker
I Had The Time of My Life - Bill Medley & Jennifer Warnes
I Ain't Got Time Anymore - Glass Bottle
It's Just a Matter of Time - Brook Benton
Long Time - Boston
Long Time Gone - Crosby, Stills & Nash

Mio Amore (My Love Til the End of Time) - Flamingos
Monkey Time - Major Lance
My Time After A While - Buddy Guy
Madison Time - Ray Bryant / Calls by Eddie Morrison
Next Time - Johnny Taylor
Next Time You See Me - Little Junior Parker
Night Time is the Right Time - Ray Charles
No Time - Guess Who
Nothing But a Good Time - Poisin
Only Time Will Tell - Asia
Part Time Love - Little Johnny Taylor
Party All the Time - Eddie Murphy
Pony Time - Chubby Checker
Right Place, Wrong Time - Otis Rush / Dr. John
Right Time of the Night - Jennifer Warnes
Sixty Minute Man - Dominoes
Take Your Time (Do It Right) - SOS Band
Too Much Time on My Hands - Styx
Turn Back The Hands of Time - Tyrone Davis
Time of the Season - Zombies
Time Warp - Rocky Horror Picture Show
This Time - Troy Shondell
Time Has Come Today - Chambers Brothers
Time is Tight - Booker T. & MGs
The Longest Time - Billy Joel
Time (Clock of the Heart) - Culture Club
Time After Time - Cyndy Lauper
Time, Love & Tenderness - Michael Bolton
Time to Get Down - O'Jays
Time Won't Let Me - Outsiders
Time is On My Side - Irma Thomas / Rolling Stones
Time in a Bottle - Jim Croce
Take Time to Know Her - Persy Sledge
The Times Thy Are A Changin' - Bob Dylan
Tomorrow is a Long Long Time - Kingston Trio
Twilight Time - Platters
Wasted Time - Eagles
What Time is It - Jive Five

& Times

Good Times - Chic
Good Times Roll - Cars
I Love You a 1000 Times - Platters
Knock Three Times - Tony Orlando & Dawn
Let The Good Times Roll - Shirley & Lee
Love Me Two Times - Doors
Three Times a Lady - Commodores / Lionel Richie
The Best of Times - Styx
Three Times a Lady - Commodores

Time - Hours, Minutes, Seconds

3/5 of a Mile in 10 Seconds - Jefferson Airplane
5-10-15 Hours - Ruth Brown
24 Hours - Eddie Boyd
24 hours from Tulsa - Gene Pitney
In the Midnight Hour - Wilson Pickett / Commitments
It Only Takes a Minute Girl - Tavares
Lovin' Every Minute of It - Loverboy
Minute By Minute - Doobie Brothers
New York Minute - Eagles / Don Henley
Sixty Minute Man - Dominoes
Three Hours Past Midnight - Johnny " Guitar " Watson
Wee Wee Hours - Chuck Berry

Tonight

Good Rockin' Tonight - Wynonie Harris / Elvis
I Wonder What She's Doing Tonight - Barry & The Tamerlanes
I Wonder What She's Doing Tonight - Tommy Boyce & Bobby Hart
I'd Really Love to See You Tonight - England Dan & John Ford Coley
Let Me Love You Tonight - Pure Prairie League
Rock Me Tonight - Billy Squier
There's A Moon Out Tonight - Capris
Tonight's All Right for Love - Elvis
Tonight I Celebrate My Love - Peabo Bryson & Roberta Flack
Tonight I Fell in Love - Tokens
Where Are You Tonight - Tom Johnston
We've Got Tonight - Bob Seger

Trains

Casey Jones - Grateful Dead
Last Train to Clarksville - Monkees
Long Train Running - Doobie Brothers
Love Train - O'Jays
Marrakesh Express - Crosby, Stills, & Nash
Midnight Train to Georgia - Gladys Knight & The Pips
Night Train - Jimmy Forrest
One Toke Over the Line - Brewer & Shipley
So Many Roads, So Many Trains - Otis Rush
Train Kept A Rollin - Johnny Burnette Trio

& Boats

Crystal Ship - Doors
Rock the Boat - Hues Corporation
Sloop John B - Beach Boys
Wreck of the Edmund Fitzgerald - Gordon Lightfoot
Wooden Ships - Crosby, Stills, & Nash

& Planes

Jet Airliner - Van Morrison
Jet Airliner - Steve Miller Band
Leaving on a Jet Plane - Peter, Paul, & Mary

Two is Company or Double Trouble

Beep Beep - Playmates
Chip Chip - Gene McDaniels
Iko Iko - Dixie Cups / Belle Stars
Hello Hello - Sopwith Camel
Hoy Hoy - Collins Kids
Liar Liar - Castaways
Louie Louie - Kingsmen
Mercy Mercy - Don Covay
Rebel Rebel - David Bowie
Sookie Sookie - Steppenwolf
Summertime Summetime - Jamies

Ta Ta - Clyde McPhatter
Talk Talk - Music Machine
Tonight Tonight - Mello Kings
Woman Woman - Gary Puckett & the Union Gap

Three's A Crowd

Cold Cold Cold - Little Feat
Cry Cry Cry - Bobby Bland
Go Go Go - Roy Orbison
Hot Hot Hot - Buster Poindexter (X - New York Doll)
Run Run Run - Supremes
Shame Shame Shame - Shirley & Co
Turn Turn Turn - Byrds
Yummy, Yummy, Yummy - Ohio Express
Zoom Zoom Zoom - Collegians

USA (Also See Patriotic)

634-5789 (Soulsville USA) - Wilson Pickett
Back in the USA - Chuck Berry
Born in the USA - Bruce Springsteen
Livin' in the USA - Steve Miller Band
R.O.C.K. in the USA - John Cougar Mellencamp
Surfin' USA - Beach Boys
Twistin' USA - Danny & The Juniors

& Other Countries

Afrika - Toto

England Swings - Roger Miller
Twistin' England - Danny & The Juniors
Next Plane to London - The Rose Garden (1967)

Mexico - James Taylor

Virgins

Can't Touch This - M.C. Hammer

Good Girl's Don't - Knack
Keep Your Hands to Yourself - Georgia Satellites
Like a Virgin - Madonna

Walking

25 Miles - Edwin Starr
A Walk in the Black Forest - Horst Jankowski (1965)
A Walkin' Miracle - Essex
Cross Tie Walker - CCR
I Want to Walk You Home - Fats Domino
I Just Can't Walk Away - Four Tops
I Walk the Line - Johnny Cash & The Tennesee Two
I'm Walkin' - Fats Domino / Ricky Nelson
I'm Walking Behind You - Eddie Fisher
I'm Gonna Let My Heart Do the Walking - Supremes
Remember (Walking in the Sand) - Shangi-Las
Sleepwalk - Santo & Johnny
Sleepwalker - Kinks
Slow Walk - Sil Austin
The Way I Walk - Jack Scott
The Walk - Jimmy McCracklin
These Boots Are Made for Walkin' - Nancy Sinatra
Walk a Mile in My Shoes - Joe South
Walk Away from Love - David Ruffin
Walk Away Renee - Left Banke / Four Tops
Walk Don't Run - Ventures
Walk Like a Man - Four Seasons
Walk Like An Egyptian - Bangles
Walk On By - Dionne Warwick
Walk of Life - Dire Straits
Walk on the Wild Side - Lou Reed
Walk on Water - Aerosmith
Walk the Dinosaur - Was (Not Was)
Walk This Way - Aerosmith / Run DMC
Walk Right Back - Everly Brothers
Walkin' Blues - Eric Clapton
Walkin' with Mr.Lee -Lee Allen & His Band
Walkin' in Memphis - Marc Cohen
Walkin' the Blues - Champion Jack Dupree

Walkin' in the Rain - Crystals / Jay & The Americans
Walkin' After Midnight - Patsy Cline
Walking By Myself - Jimmy Rogers
Walking on Sunshine - Katrina & The Waves (1985)
Walking on the Moon - Police
Walking the Dog - Rufus Thomas
Walking Along - Solitaires
Walking in Rhythmn - Blackbyrds
Walking to New Orleans - Fats Domino
You'll Never Walk Alone - Righteous Brothers

War

Ballad of the Green Berets - Sgt. Barry Sadler
Battle of New Orleans - Johnny Preston
Battle of Kookamonga - Homer & Jethro
Born in the USA - Bruce Springsteen
Deck of Cards - Wink Martindale
In the Navy - Village People
Navy Blue - Diane Renay
Life After Wartime - Talking Heads
Lucky Man - Emerson, Lake & Palmer
One Tin Soldier (The Legend of Billie Jack) - Coven (1970)
Sky Pilot - Eric Burdon & The Animals
Soldier Boy - Shirelles

& Peace

Alice's Restaurant - Arlo Guthrie
Eve of Destruction - Barry Maguire
For What It's Worth - Buffalo Springfield
Fortunate Son - CCR
Get Together - Youngbloods
Give Peace a Chance - John Lennon & Yoko Ono
I Feel Like I'm Fixin' to Die Rag - Country Joe & the Fish
Something in the Air - Thunderclap Newman
Unknown Soldier - Doors
War - Edwin Starr

& International Intrigue (One of My More Creative)

All Along the Watchtower - Bob Dylan / Jimi Hendrix
All She Wants to Do is Dance - Don Henley
Bette Davis Eyes - Kim Carnes
Der Kommisar - After the Fire
It's the End of the World as We Know It - R.E.M.
Lawyers, Guns, & Money - Warren Zevon
Life After Wartime - Talking Heads
Lunatic Fringe - Red Ryder
Secret Agent Man - Johnny Rivers
Silent Running - Mike & The Mechanics
Smuggler's Blues - Glenn Frey
Someone's Watching Me - Rockwell
Something in the Air - Thunderclap Newman (1969)
Third Man Theme - Anton Karas

& 007

Live & Let Die - Paul McCartney
Goldfinger - Shirley Bassey
Nobody Does It Better - Carly Simon
007 Theme - John Williams

Weather

Bad Weather - Supremes
Lightning Strikes - Lou Christie
Like the Weather - 10,000 Maniacs
Storm Warning - Volcanoes
Stormy Weather - Spaniels / Magnificent Men
Stormy Monday Blues - Bobby Bland
Storm Front - Billy Joel

& Wind Songs

Against the Wind - Bob Seger
Blowing in the Wind - Bob Dylan / Peter, Paul, & Mary / Joan Baez
Blowing Kisses in the Wind - Paula Abdul
Candle in the Wind - Elton John

Catch the Wind - Donovan
Dust in the Wind - Kansas
Free as the Wind - Johnny Maestro & The Brooklyn Bridge
Let the Four Winds Blow - Fats Domino
Mandolin Wind - Rod Stewart
Ride Like the Wind - Christopher Cross
Sailing the Wind - Loggins & Messina
She's Like the Wind - Patrick Swayse
Summer Breeze - Seals & Crofts
Summer Wind - Frank Sinatra
Wind Cries Mary - Jimi Hendrix
Wind Beneath My Wings - Bette Midler
Wayward Wind - Gogi Grant
Windy - Association

& Rain Songs

Another Rainy Day in New York City - Chicago
Here Comes That Rainy Day Feeling Again - Fortunes
I Can't Stand the Rain - Commitments
I Wish It Would Rain -Temptations
I Think It's Going to Rain Today - Joe Cocker
In the Rain - Dramatics
It's Raining Men - Weather Girls
Lightning Strikes - Lou Christie
Let It Rain - Eric Clapton
Mandolin Rain - Bruce Hornsby & The Range
Purple Rain - Prince
Rainy Day Bells - Globetrotters (Basketball Legends)
Raindrops - Dee Clark
Raindrops Keep Falling on My Head - B.J. Thomas
Rain on the Roof - Lovin' Spoonful
Rainin' in My Heart - Slim Harpo
Red Rain - Peter Gabriel
Rythmn of the Rain - Cascades
Sun Ain't Gonna Shine Anymore - Walker Brothers
Tell It to the Rain - Four Seasons
When the Rain Comes - Beatles
Who'll Stop the Rain - CCR

& Sun Songs

A Place in the Sun - Stevie Wonder / Four Tops
California Sun - Rivieras
Here Comes the Sun - Beatles
I Live for the Sun - Sunrays
Sunny - Bobby Hebb
Sun Ain't Gonna Shine Anymore - Walker Brothers
Sunshine of Your Love - Cream
Please Mr. Sun - Johnny Ray
Warmth of the Sun - Beach Boys
You Are the Sunshine of My Life - Stevie Wonder

Wild Wild West

Ballad of Davey Crockett - Bill Hayes
Cisco Kid - War
Cowboys to Girls - Intruders
Come a Little Bit Closer - Jay & Americans
Desperado - Eagles / Linda Ronstadt
El Paso - Marty Robbins
Good, Bad & The Ugly - Hugo Montenegro
Happy Trails to You - Roy Rogers & Dale Evans
I Shot the Sheriff - Eric Clapton
Long Tall Texan - Murry Kellum
Man Who Shot Liberty Valence - Gene Pitney
Mr. Custer - Larry Verne
Mule Skinner Blues - Fendermen
Rawhide - Link Wray & His Raymen
Reverend Mr. Black - Johnny Cash / Kingston Trio
Rhinestone Cowboy - Glen Campbell
Wild Wild West - Escape Club

WILD!

Born to Be Wild - Steppenwolf
Ride the Wild Surf - Jan & Dean
Walk on the Wild Side - Lou Reed
Wild Boys - Duran Duran
Wild Hearts - Roy Orbison

Wild Night - Van Morrison
Wild Night - John Cougar Mellencamp
Wild Thing - Troggs
Wild Weekend - Rockin' Rebels
Wild Honey - Beach Boys
Wild Horses - Rolling Stones
Wild Mountain Honey - Steve Miller Band
Wild World - Cat Stevens
Wildfire - Michael Martin Murphey
Wildwood Days - Bobby Rydell
Wildwood Boogie - Charlie Gracie
Wildwood Weed - Jim Stafford
Wildest Dreams - Asia
Your Wildest Dreams - Moody Blues

Wine Songs

Bottle of Wine - Jimmy Gilmer & The Fireballs
Chug A Lug - Roger Miller
Drinkin' Wine Spo-Dee-Oh-Dee - Smiley Lewis / Jerry Lee Lewis /
Charlie Burnett Trio
Red Red Wine - UB40
Sweet Cherry Wine - Tommy James & The Shondells
Spill the Wine - Eric Burdon & War
White Port & Lemon Juice - Bel Aires

& Other Spirits

Bad Bad Whiskey - Amos Milburn
Boat Drinks - Jimmy Buffet
I Drink Alone - George Thorogood & The Delaware Destroyers
Let Me Go Home Whiskey - Amos Milburn
Margaritaville - Jimmy Buffet
Moonlight Cocktails - Rivieras
One Mint Julep - Clovers
One Bourbon, One Scotch & One Beer - Amos Milburn & His Chicken
Shackers / George Thorogood & The Delaware Destroyers
Tequila - Champs
Tequila Sunrise - Eagles
Whiskey in a Jar - Clancy Brothers / Metallica

Whiskey Train - Procul Harem

Wizard of Oz (Listener Suggested - Lions & Tigers & Bears, Oh My)

Be My Teddy Bear - Elvis
Ding Dong the Witch is Dead - Fifth Estate
Goodbye Yellow Brick Road - Elton John
Lion Sleeps Tonight - Tokens / Robert John / Kingston Trio
Somewhere Over the Rainbow - Little Anthony & The Imperials
Tiger - Fabian

Woman

A Woman Needs Love (Just Like I Do) - Ray Parker Jr. & Raydio
Ain't No Woman (Like The One I've Got) - Four Tops
Along Comes a Woman - Chicago
American Woman - Guess Who
Black Magic Woman - Fleetwood Mac / Santana
Black Country Woman - Led Zeppelin
Clean Up Woman - Betty Knight
Do Right Woman, Do Right Man - Aretha Franklin / Commitments
Devil Woman - Cliff Richard
Evil Woman Don't Play Your Games with Me - Crow
Evil Woman - ELO
Get Out of My Life Woman - Lee Dorsey
Gypsy Woman - Impressions / Four Seasons
Hard Headed Woman - Elvis
Hard headed Woman - Cat Stevens
Have You Ever Loved a Woman - Freddy King
Half a Woman, Half a Shadow - Roxette
Honky Tonk Woman - Rolling Stones
I Am Woman - Helen Reddy
I Can Love You Like a Woman - Koko Taylor
I Got a Woman - Ray Charles
I'm Every Woman - Whitney Houston
If I Were Your Woman - Gladys Knight & The Pips
It's a Man Down There - G.I. Crockett
I'm Every Woman - Chaka Khan
If I Were Your Woman - Aretha Franklin
Kentucky Woman - Deep Purple

L.A. Woman - Doors
Long Cool Woman (In a Black Dress) - Hollies
Love Makes a Woman - Barbara Acklin
No Woman No Cry - Bob Marley & The Wailers
Oh Pretty Woman - Roy Orbison
She's Not Just Another Woman - 8th Day
She's a Woman - Beatles
She's Always a Woman - Billy Joel
This Girl is a Woman Now - Gary Pluckett & The Union Gap
The Other Woman - Ray Parker Jr.
We've Got to Get You a Woman - Boyce & Hart
When your in Love with a Beautiful Woman - Dr. Hook
We Gotta Get You a Woman - Runt / Todd Rundgren
When a Man Loves a Woman - Percy Sledge / Michael Bolton
Woman to Woman - Shirley Brown / Joe Cocker
Woman's Love Rights - Laura Lee
Woman's Gotta have It - Bobby Womack
You Are the Woman - Firefall
You Make Me Feel (Like a Natural Woman) - Aretha Franklin

Your Best Friend's Girl

Girl of My Best Friend - Ral Donner
Jesse's Girl - Rick Springfield
Marie's the Name (Of His Latest Flame) - Elvis
My Best Friend's Girl - Cars

Your Cheatin' Heart

It's My Party - Leslie Gore
I Shot Mr. Lee - Bobbettes
Lipstick on Your Collar - Connie Francis
Me & Mrs. Jones - Billy Paul
Ruby, Don't Take Your Love to Town - Kenny Rogers
Something on Your Mind - Big Jay McNeely / Bobby Marchan
Take a Letter Marie - R.B. Greaves
The Other Woman - Ray Parker Jr. & Raydio
Trying to Love Two - William Bell (1977)
Who' Makin' Love - Johnny Taylor
Who's Cheatin' Who - Little Milton

Your Cheatin' Heart - Hank Williams
Handyman - Jimmy Jones / James Taylor

ZZZZZZ's

Endless Sleep - Jodie sands
I'm Only Sleeping - Beatles
Oh Lord, I Wish I Could Sleep - Spinners
Sleepwalk - Santo & Johnny
Sleeping Bag - Z Z Top
Sleeping with the Television On - Billie Joel
Sleepwalker - Kinks
Somebody's Been Sleeping - 100 Proof Aged in Soul
Talking in Your Sleep - Romantics / Crystal Gayle
The Lion Sleeps Tonight - Tokens / Robert John / Kingston Trio

A Very Brief History of Rock & Roll (In the Beginning, Fifties & Beyond)

Rock & Roll was the bastard child of Southern Blues Shouting, known in
the 40's & 50's as "Race" Music & Country & Western derived "Rockabilly" !!!

Rock & Roll (Rawk and Roll) the term first used by Cleveland Ohio Disk
Jockey Alan Freed in the early Fifties for his *Moondog Rock & Roll Party*
probably taken from The Song " My Baby Rocks Me with a Steady Roll " also
prominently featured in Bill Haley & His Comets rendition of " Rock The Joint "
We're Gonna Rock, We're Gonna Roll.The phrases Rock, Roll & Rock & Roll
were traditionally used in Blues, the foundation of this new music, as *hipster*
slang for Sexual Intercourse. No wonder it was considered the devil's music
& had church leaders preaching against it & burning records !!!

The very first Rock & Roll record is reported to be **"Rocket 88"** by Ike Turner
& His Rythmn Kings credited to Jackie Brenston the man with the soulful sax
solo. Ike was to later to hook up with Anna Mae Bullock from Nutbush, Tenn
& form "Ike & Tina Turner". The Dawn of the Rock & Roll Age really started
when the Bill Haley & His Comets song **"Rock Around the Clock"** was
featured over the credits of the 1955 movie "Blackboard Jungle" starring Glenn
Ford, as an idealistic teacher coping with rebellious teenagers Vic Morrow &
Sidney Portier in an inner city school.The song written in late 1952 was first
performed at the Hof Brau in Wildwood By the Sea, NJ (*Now you know the
true birthplace of Rock & Roll*). **Rock Around the Clock** was later recorded

by Haley in 1954 on the heals of his big hit "Crazy Man Crazy" & became the first Rock & Roll Record to top the American Pop Charts in Cashbox, Billboard & other music charts all around the World. His Comets were his Court & Bill Haley was the first true unheralded "King of Rock & Roll"

The electric guitar became the instrument of choice & Chuck Berry was it's master blaster. What young guitarist wasn't inspired by the riffs in Johnny B. Goode ? True Inspiration ! Bass provided the bottom end & drums were added for that steady back beat. The holy instrument trinity was ordained.

R & B artists who were covered during the early days by white wannabes, started to take their rightful place on the charts. Street corner harmonies took hold with groups like the Frankie Lymon & the Teenagers & The Penguins. The Platters dominated the soulful side & Fats Domino was a force to be reckoned with. The Crests, with Johnny Maestro, became the first racially integrated group. The Drifters brought orchestral arrangements to pop, then Clyde McPhatter went solo. The Coasters, Little Richard, & Jerry Lee Lewis. had "Wild & Crazy" all sewn up & Pat Boone kept the Twixt Twelve & Twenti homogenized. The beginnings of Rock & Roll. Alan Freed's Radio Show moved from Cleveland to New York & he continued to spin his favs. His "Sol Out " Rock & Roll Shows featured them all. It was the Best of Both Worlds!!!

"King" Haley was dethroned by that hip swinging hearthrob Elvis the Pelvis as Colonel Parker's Sensation began to dominate the airwaves, & after all a balding middle age rocker with a spit curl in the middle of his forehead didn't fit the image of an industry driven by teenage lust ,angst, & rebellion. The ne Teen Idols like Elvis Presley, Ricky Nelson, Paul Anka, Bobby Rydell, Franki Avalon, & Fabian ruled the roost & drove the little girls, W-I-L-D! Connie Francis, & Annette Funicello, showed that the ladies could hold their own too

Teens danced to the Jukebox at the soda shoppe, & at "At the Hop" in black slacks & white bucks, poodle skirts & saddle shoes. Rock & Roll was Here to Stay, Dick Clark's American Bandstand in The City of Brotherly Lovesville made sure of that !!! It went Coast to Coast every afternoon after school.

Doo Wop, Girl Groups, Surf Music, & the Motown Sound. all had their turns a immortality, until the Beatles & the British Invasion turned the music scene o it's ear once again. Rock & Roll was constantly evolving. Revolution & Evolution, and they said it was just a FAD ...... Baby, The Beat Goes On !!!
~ Scott Alan Murphy 2007 ~

The Soundtrack of My Life - Scott Alan Murphy

Songs that have a special significance to me, define my generation,
& tell my life story in song!!!

From Conception to the Grave ....

Birthday - Beatles
Theme from Leave It to Beaver
Take Five - Dave Brubeck
MTA - Kingston Trio
Blowing in the Wind - Peter, Paul & Mary
Walk Don't Run - Ventures
Bandstand Boogie - Les & Larry Elgart / Barry Manilow
Rock Around the Clock - Bill Haley & His Comets
At the Hop - Danny & the Juniors
Rockin' Robin - Bobby Day
Chantilly Lace - Big Bopper
Gloria - Van Morrison / Shadows of Knight
Happy Days - Pratt & McClain
Be True to Your School - Beach Boys
Twist - Chubby Checker (The first song I ever danced to)
Louie Louie - Kingsmen
If You Wanna Be Happy - Jimmy Soul
Another Brick in the Wall - Pink Floyd
Girl Watcher - O'Kaysion
Hey Little Girl - Dee Clark
Dobie Gray - In Crowd
Do You Love Me - Contours
Land of a Thousand Dances - Cannibal & The Headhunters / Wilson Pickett
Footloose - Kenny Loggins
Going to A Go Go - Smokey Robinson
Jordan Brothers Theme - Jordan Brothers
Bristol Stomp - Dovells
Dirty Water - Standells
Sleepwalk - Santo & Johnny
What's Your Name - Don & Juan
Heart - Jordan Brothers
Image of a Girl - Surfaris
Satisfaction - Rolling Stones

Mony Mony - Tommy James & The Shondells
Born to Be Wild - Steppenwolf
Ride Like The Wind - Christopher Cross
Solsbury Hill - Peter Gabriel
Times They Are A'Changin' - Bob Dylan
Like a Rolling Stone - Bob Dylan
The Weight - The Band
One Toke Over the Line - Brewer & Shipley
Ina Gadda Da Vida - Iron Butterfly (Long Version - 19 minutes)
Incense & Peppermints - Strawberry Alarm Clock
Time Has Come Today - Chambers Brothers
White Rabbit - Jefferson Airplane
Journey to the Center of Your Mind - Amboy Dukes
Sunshine of Your Love - Cream
I Am the Walrus - Beatles
Something In the Air - Buffalo Springfield
All Along the Watchtower - Jimi Hendrix / Bob Dylan
Eve of Destruction - Barry MaGuire
Sympathy for the Devil - Rolling Stones
War - Edwin Starr
Fortunate Sun - CCR
Get Together - Youngbloods
Lucky Man - Emerson, Lake & Palmer
Suite Judy Blue Eyes - Crosby, Stills & Nash
Scheherazade - Renaissance
Night Moves - Bob Seger
Feel Like Makin' Love - Bad Company
Go All the Way - Rasberries
Aqualung - Jethro Tull
Whole Lotta Love - Led Zeppelin
You Shook Me All Night Long - AC DC
All Day & All of the Night - Kinks
Teacher - Jethro Tull
Born to Run - Bruce Springsteen
Down the Shore - Crystal Mansion
Wildwood Days - Bobby Rydell
Brown Eyed Girl - Van Morrison
Heatwave - Martha & the Vandellas
Wipeout - Sufaris
Live for the Sun - Sunrays

Baba O'Reilly - Who
Layla - Cream / Eric Clapton (The Electric Version)
You Keep Me Hanging On - Supremes / Vanilla Fudge
Hey Little Girl - Syndicate of Sound
The Chain - Fleetwood Mac
Go Your Own Way - Fleetwood Mac
Stand Back - Stevie Nicks
Disco Inferno - Trammps
Bad Girls / Hot Stuff - Donna Summer
Dancing Queen - ABBA
Do You Wanna Funk - Sylvester
Please Don't Let Me Be Misunderstood - Animals / Santa Esmeralda
Freeze Frame - J. Geils Band
Jack & Diane - John Cougar Mellencamp
Pop Music - M
Life is a Rock - Reunion
Rock On - David Essex
Money for Nothing - Dire Straits
Old Time Rock & Roll - Bob Seger
Havin' A Party - Sam Cooke / Southside Johnny & the Asbury Jukes
A Well Respected Man - Kinks
Money - Barrett Strong
Oh Carol - Neil Sedaka
I Love You - People
Hot for Teacher - Van Halen
This Magic Moment - Drifters / Jay & the Americans
Be My Baby - Ronettes
When A Man Loves A Woman - Percy Sledge
It's Now or Never - Elvis Presley
Chapel of Love - Dixie Cups
Soul & Inspiration - Righteous Brothers
She's Always A Woman - Billy Joel
Tell It Like It Is - Aaron Neville
Games People Play - Joe South
I Heard It Through The Grapevine - Marvin Gaye
Ain't Too Proud To Beg - Temptations
You've Lost That Lovin' Feeling - Righteous Brothers
Liar Liar - Castaways
Sgt. Pepper's Lonely Hearts Club Band - Beatles
Shake Me, Wake Me When It's Over - Four Tops

It's Over - Roy Orbison
I'm Gonna Be Strong - Gene Pitney
Only the Strong Survive - Jerry Butler
What Becomes of the Broken Hearted - Jimmy Ruffin
Owner of a Lonely Heart - Yes
Celebration - Kool & the Gang
9 to 5 - Dolly Parton
Kokomo - Beach Boys
For the Love of Money - O'Jays
I'm Free - Who
Come On Down to My Boat - Every Mother's Son
Sailing - Christopher Cross
Sea Cruise - Frankie Ford
Montego Bay - Bobby Bloom / Amazulu
Cheeseburger in Paradise - Jimmy Buffet
Margaritaville - Jimmy Buffet
We Be Jammin' - Bob Marley
One Love - Bob Marley
Glory Days - Bruce Springsteen
Touch of Grey - Grateful Dead
When I'm Sixty Four- Beatles
Don't Fear The Reaper - Blue Oyster Cult
People Get Ready - Impressions
Spirit in the Sky - Norman Greenbaum
Dust in the Wind - Kansas

Last Will & Testament

This book is my way of leaving something behind, The Music & The
Memories !!! When the Time Comes .... Have a PARTY instead of a
Funeral. Tell Lies About Me, & *Spin These Tunes* in the order they appear
on the list. Celebrate my life & remember me as A Professor of Musicology
& DJ Extraordinaire !!! That's how I'd like to transcend to the next level !!!

..................Thanx, Scott

FUN with Oldies
~ Scott Alan Murphy ~

A Book of Lists of Oldies & Classic Rock Songs
Categorized by Idea, Genre, or Theme
Over 180 Categories of Your Favorite Songs
"A Special Addition to Any Oldies Library"

There are probably some cosmic connections & selections
in these collections, that have missed my recollections!.
~
Therefore
If you have any categories
you think I should add
any suggestions
or you just want to comment on the book
Please
e-mail me
Scott Alan Murphy
mindzwarped@hotmail.com
funwitholdies@hotmail.com
Web Page http://www.devoted.to/oldies
MSN or Yahoo Mesenger: mindzwarped@hotmail.com
To Order CD Copies funwitholdies@hotmail.com
Additional Books: Lulu.com/Oldies
& Amazon.com
on the Weird Wide Web
& select Retail Outlets
Ask your local bookstore to stock it
if you don't see it!!!
~
Keep Rockin' & Rollin'
It's the Only Way to Fly

"Rock & Roll is Here to Stay" - Danny & the Juniors
~
Not the End ~ Only the Beginning
~